The Balkan (

Travels around the Former Yugoslavia....

By Jason Smart

Published by Smart Travel Publishing

Text and Photographs © 2013 Jason Smart

All Right Reserved. No part of this book may be reproduced or transmitted in any form or by any means, electronic or mechanical, including photocopying, recording, or any information storage and retrieval system, without prior written permission of the Author.

For the people of the Balkans

Bled
SLOVENIA
ROMANIA
Porec
SERBIA
Belgrade
BOSNIA and HERZEGOVINA
Sarajevo
CROATIA
Mostar
KOSOVO
Dubrovnik
Kotor
Pristina
MONTENEGRO
Skopje
MACEDONIA
ITALY
Tirana
Ohrid
ALBANIA
GREECE

Table of contents

1. Belgrade, Serbia 1

2. Sarajevo, Bosnia & Herzegovina................................21

3. Porec, Croatia 41

4. Bled, Slovenia 51

5. Dubrovnik, Croatia 61

6. Mostar, Bosnia & Herzegovina...................................75

7. Kotor, Montenegro 89

8. Tirana, Albania 97

9. Ohrid, Macedonia 115

10. Skopje: Macedonia..125

11. Pristina, Kosovo 143

Afterword...165

1. Belgrade, Serbia

Interesting fact: Serbia is the world's largest exporter of raspberries.

"Okay," said Phil, "where's next on your travel hit list?"

I'd been friends with Phil for over twenty years, ever since we'd met at university. He looked at me and took a sip of his lager. My other friend Michael watched me too, a light smile on his face. He already knew the answer.

Phil simply couldn't understand my fascination with visiting foreign lands. To him, a week in Spain or a fortnight in Portugal was the basis of a good holiday, and the prospect of jetting off to some weird country in Eastern Europe was an alien concept. Michael was different though – he understood my need completely. In fact, Michael and I had already done a bit of travelling together. We had once travelled from Bucharest to Kiev.

"The Balkans," I told Phil. "That's the next region on the list."

Phil put his drink down, but kept his expression neutral. "The Balkans?"

I nodded. "Yes, the Balkans." Michael's smile turned into a grin.

"As in Bulgaria and Greece?"

"Yes, as in Bulgaria and Greece. But we're concentrating on the former countries of Yugoslavia."

Phil's eyes widened as he looked at Michael. "...So you're already in on this plan of Jason's?"

Michael nodded. "I've always fancied going to Belgrade."

Phil picked up his drink and shook his head.

"And, after Belgrade," I said to Phil, "we're going to fly to Bosnia, and then Croatia. After that, we'll play it by ear, but we want to visit Albania and Macedonia at some point. Hopefully Slovenia, too."

Phil looked up. "I didn't think Albania was part of Yugoslavia."

"I know," I said. "But our route takes us through it. Besides, who wouldn't want to visit Albania?"

"Me," said Phil. "And most other people." He turned to Michael. "Do you really want to go to Albania?"

Michael nodded.

"Anyway," I said. "We also want to go to Montenegro and Kosovo."

"Kosovo! What are you both, bloody pretend peacekeepers? Where are you going to buy your bullet-proof vests from?"

"So you don't fancy joining us?" joked Michael.

Phil replaced his drink on the table. He didn't even bother to answer the question.

2

"Where are you boys off to?" asked the man sitting at our table. With a rush of early-morning passengers, the restaurants at Manchester Airport were almost full to capacity. The lack of tables had forced the man to join us. He was wearing a business suit, and was aged about fifty. Like Michael and me, he had a full English breakfast, a hearty meal for any traveller.

"Serbia and then Bosnia," answered Michael, cutting his sausage in half.

The man looked us up and down. "Bosnia? Are you two in the forces?"

I shook my head and was just about to explain, but the man spoke first. "Please don't tell me you're going there on holiday?"

Michael smiled. "Well, yes. We're visiting the whole Balkan region. Serbia and Bosnia are just the start."

The man shook his head. "Do you know something? I've flown down to London every week for about three years now. Whenever I get the chance, I ask people where they're going. You're the first people who've said Bosnia."

In the aftermath of World War One, the Kingdom of Yugoslavia came into being. Prior to that, the region was composed of different Slavic nations (including Serbia, Croatia and Slovenia), all of them sick and tired of foreign occupation. They decided to unite. A series of kings ruled the country until the Axis powers invaded in 1941. The royal family escaped to London just in time.

The Nazis took over the region and began to round up, and then murder, tens of thousands of Jews. Then they started doing the same thing to Serbian civilians, especially those they believed to be communists or Roma. The communists, in particular, were causing problems for the Nazis, because many of them had formed into rebel units. They became such an irritation, the Germans came up with a plan: for every German soldier wounded in battle, they would execute fifty Yugoslav communists; for each German soldier killed in battle, a hundred would die.

When communist partisans killed ten German soldiers, and wounded twenty-six more, the price, a Nazi commander worked out, was 2300 deaths. German forces moved into the city of Kragujevac (now in modern-day Serbia), and rounded up every Jewish male they could find. This only amounted to 70 men, well below the quota required, so the Germans simply gathered every male between the age of 16 and 60 to make up numbers. At 6pm that night, the executions began. Soldiers shot 400 men at a time, and the killings did not stop until thousands of Serbs lay dead.

Despite this, partisan attacks on German units continued. Eventually, they reached such a level that the Germans retreated, leaving Yugoslavia in the hands of communist freedom fighters. One of the first things the communists did was abolish the monarchy, and change the name of the country. Instead of the Kingdom of Yugoslavia, it became the Socialist Federal Republic of Yugoslavia. The head of the new government was one of the communist rebel leaders. His name was Josip Tito.

After getting our passports stamped, Michael and I walked into the arrivals hall of Belgrade International Airport. The flight from Manchester had been straightforward, involving a brief stopover in Frankfurt before boarding a JAT Airways flight (the national airline of Serbia) to Belgrade.

Almost immediately after entering the arrivals hall, the taxi drivers set upon us – a pack of thick-moustached men in leather jackets and jeans, all asking if we wanted a ride to Belgrade centre. Ignoring them, Michael and I sought refuge in the airport bar. We needed to locate a prepaid phone to order an official airport taxi. As we sipped our first Serbian beers, I consulted the guidebook. "You'll never guess what," I said, shaking my head in annoyance.

"What?" Michael replied.

"We should've rung for a taxi *before* passport control. The phones were back there."

Michael nodded. Hardly any situation fazed him. In fact, he was one the calmest people I knew. "What about a bus?" he asked. "Because there's one outside now."

I flicked through the guidebook searching for bus information, turning pages until I found what I was looking for. "You're right. It says a bus leaves every hour, on the hour."

We both simultaneously glanced at our watches and saw it was 7pm. We swivelled our heads and looked outside to see the bus move away from the terminal. Our only means of cheap escape had gone.

I threw my head back and sighed. There was nothing we could do except wait for another bus in an hour's time. But neither of us could be bothered with that. We finished our beers and walked back into the arrival hall. We stood in the middle like antelope waiting for the first bite. It took about ten seconds.

"Ah, you boys want taxi?" said a deep voice. Dark hair, in his thirties, the man tried to disarm us with a smile. "I take you to centre very quick. You not get any cheaper. And look, bus has gone!" He grinned at his observation.

After establishing the price (40 euros), we followed the taxi driver outside. At least the weather was nice. Even though it was only April, Belgrade was pleasantly warm and sunny.

5

"You Americano?" the taxi driver asked as he turned onto the main highway. Agricultural fields near the airport quickly gave way to residential buildings - mostly tall houses with dramatically sloping roofs. Michael told the driver we were from the UK, a town near Manchester.

The man grinned. "Ah! Manchester United! Good football team!"

Everywhere in the world, it seemed, from the jungles of Borneo, to the temples of Peru, people knew about English football, and especially Manchester United. After a quick conversation about how well Wayne Rooney was doing, the taxi driver asked us why we were in Belgrade.

"We're tourists," said Michael.

The driver glanced back and nodded. Outside, apartment blocks had replaced the tall houses. We'd reached the outskirts of the Serbian capital.

"This is River Danube," the man said as we crossed a long bridge. "If you look up there, you can see fortress on hill. Very nice place. You must go there. Very good."

The fortress was already on our list of places to visit in Belgrade. Michael was especially interested in it because of a fortress museum he'd read about.

We reached the other side of the bridge, where the buildings looked older and grander, perhaps dating from when the Hapsburgs were in charge. Ten minutes later, we pulled up in Stari Grad,

Belgrade's old town, and paid the taxi fee. Country number one of the Balkan Odyssey was about to begin.

6

It was just past eight in the evening. Michael and I sat down under a large parasol, enjoying a Jelen Pivo, the local beer. I regarded a busy street to our left. A red tram was trundling along, as was a taxi, prowling for business. A pair of young women laughed as they sauntered past a shop splashed with Cyrillic. They looked dressed for a night in one of Belgrade's famous hot spots.

"I'm starving," Michael announced. I was hungry too, and picked up a menu, but couldn't understand a word because it was in Cyrillic. Instead, I looked at the food on the next table. Two men were tucking into what looked like chipolata sausages stuffed inside pita bread. Whatever it was, they were loving it. "I'm going to have what they've got," I said. Michael nodded in agreement.

When the waitress came over, I slyly pointed at the food on the next table, and held up two fingers. She nodded and turned tail. Ten minutes later, our meals arrived, and were as tasty as promised. It *was* spiced sausages of some kind, but with another meat, possibly lamb. And it was so cheap. Afterwards, we headed off towards Belgrade Fortress as dusk began to settle over the city.

7

Situated on a high rocky ridge, Belgrade Fortress looked out over the confluence of River Danube and River Sava. It consisted of stony battlements and medieval-looking round towers. In 1979, the Yugoslav government declared it a *Monument of Exceptional Importance*.

Initially, the population of Belgrade had lived inside the fortress. The high walls kept them safe from the barbarian hordes outside. But then the Romans came knocking and took over the fort. While they were in town, they fought off invasions by the

Goths and the Huns, causing all manners of sieges and standoffs in the process. But the fortress survived, and was altered and added to, and then became centre stage in a world-shattering event.

In 1914, a Serbian called Gavrilo Princip killed an Austrian Archduke in Sarajevo. The Austrians were mad as hell, and stationed an artillery unit on the other side of the river from Belgrade fort. When the Austrians eventually fired upon it, they effectively started the hostilities of World War I.

Michael and I clambered up a pathway until we arrived at the fortress gate, a stony archway flanked by round towers. Once inside, we climbed to one of the highest points of the complex, up on the battlements, a place offering a great view.

"Not bad," said Michael as we stared out across the Danube. "Not bad at all."

All along the wall, and in the parkland adjoining it, were groups of teenagers. Some were sipping cans of lager, while others were enjoying ice creams. Some kids were kissing and canoodling, but most were just chatting. These Serbian teenagers seemed carefree, happy to be out in the evening sun. We left them to their twilight sojourn, and climbed back down. As the lights came on, and the party people of Belgrade came out in force, Michael and I returned to the hotel. It had been a long day.

8

The next morning, after breakfast, Michael and I walked to Republic Square, him leading the way as usual. I'd already discovered that Michael had one of those special talents that enabled him to look at a map and immediately memorise everything on it. His skill was almost intuitive, if not downright spooky, but I'd quickly learned not to question his directional abilities; he was seldom wrong.

Republic Square was large and busy, with people rushing hither and thither as they went about their business. Smoke-belching cars, plodding trucks, and overweight buses and trams were using the square as a major transit point. Michael and I crossed the road to reach the middle.

Before the square had existed, the Turks had used it as a place of execution. They impaled non-Muslims on large spikes if they refused to sway their beliefs. Nowadays though, Republic Square looked very European, lined with grand buildings, including the National Theatre and National Museum.

"What is it about men on horses?" I said, staring up at a statue of a warrior sitting atop his steed. "They all look the same, and nearly every city has one. I bet this bloke didn't even have a horse. Who is he anyway? And why is he pointing like that?"

"He was a nineteenth-century Serbian Prince," answered Michael, using his encyclopaedic knowledge of history. "And I think he managed to get rid of the Turks from Serbia. He's pointing towards Constantinople."

I spun around to see where he was pointing now. It was at a massive six-storey building with a large *Jugoexport* sign on the top. How times had changed.

9

Skadarlija is the famous bohemian area of Belgrade. The long, winding cobbled streets attract tourists because of the numerous antique shops and moody art galleries.

Skadarlija's history began in the 1830s when a group of Roma gypsies settled in the area. With their loutish and unkempt ways, they soon made the district a no-go area.

Twenty years later, Skadarlija was overrun with Roma, and so the authorities sprang into action. They advanced through the hovels, expelling everyone in their path, threatening those who refused to budge with prison (or worse). This hardline tactic worked well and the Roma families left. Brick buildings replaced decrepit homes, and artisans and craftsmen moved into them. As time passed, writers and actors came to stay, and then distinguished families took up residence. Skadarlija became the hippest area of downtown Belgrade.

One famous resident had been Dura Jaksic, a nineteenth-century poet, painter, and patriot. After studying fine art in Vienna, Jaksic had abandoned his paintings to join a revolution. Unfortunately, the transition from paintbrush to musket was not a wise decision, because he was wounded in battle. Once recovered, he gave up soldiering and settled in Skadarlija to become a bohemian. He was well known for inviting other painters, writers, and actors into his abode for nights of frivolity.

Michael and I stared at the bronze statue of Jaksic outside the building that had presumably been his home. Sat on a plinth, gazing upwards in deep poetic thought, Jaksic looked a bit dishevelled. His bearded face, loose clothes and large hat gave him the appearance of someone at a low point in their life. Perhaps that's how he'd wanted to appear.

The cobbled street of Skadarlija also featured quaint outdoor eateries with green and blue chequered tablecloths. Wooden benches (complete with obligatory sleeping cats), and large barrels with plants spilling over their rims, made the area extremely pretty. Flowerpots and green shutters added bursts of colour. All Skadarlija needed were a few old men in caps, and the scene of yesteryear would be complete.

"Look," Michael said, pointing upwards. It was a set of tall buildings decorated in an interesting way. Daubed over the otherwise dull facades were colours and designs that gave the buildings the illusion of being much grander.

One building with only three windows caught my eye in particular. Due to some skilful painting, it now had nine. The building next door had a set of luscious green trees and a fetching stone archway. All a fantasy.

We stared a while, and then headed to a nearby market.

10

Bajloni Market was packed with fruit and vegetable stalls, staffed by fearsome-looking ladies. One woman patrolled a section dedicated to green apples. She sported dyed red hair and a patterned blue apron. When she caught my eye, she glared, as if daring me to approach. I looked away, wondering whether she was actually a man.

A small boy of about eight squeezed past us on a bike. Ahead of him was a crush of people, but the boy didn't care, and tried to ram his way through. Within seconds, he crashed into the side of an elderly woman. She was carrying a bag of lettuces in one hand, and a wooden cane in the other. With one swift arm movement, she clipped the boy on the head. As he attempted to ride off, she whacked him again, shouting something. Uninjured, the boy cycled off, but didn't get far. After avoiding a collision with a carrot stall, he crashed into the back of another woman, this one younger. After yelping, she spun around and gave the boy a hard shove, causing him to topple from his bike. He simply climbed back on and pedalled away, soon becoming lost in the crowds.

At the other side of the market, we came across a pitiful sight. It was a young dark-haired woman fast asleep in a doorway. How she slept in the heat and noise we couldn't fathom, but what made it worse were her two children. A small boy and girl were huddled next to the woman, also asleep, both wearing next to nothing. They looked like Roma.

Serbia has one of the largest Roma populations in Europe, with unofficial estimates putting the number at half a million. Mostly the Roma live in slum conditions at the edges of Serbian cities, but in Belgrade, they live in the centre too. With no running water or electricity, the Roma people are forced to scavenge for water, and must burn rubbish for warmth. Often life is so hard for them that many end up begging on the streets for money.

In 2009, things came to a head in a Belgrade slum nicknamed Cardboard City, home to almost a thousand people. Serbian authorities waded in and cleared the area, re-housing some families, but deporting others back to their country of origin. Mostly though, ousted families were forced into living on the streets.

Michael and I dropped a few coins on the woman's blanket and moved on, wondering how people like her lived in such deplorable conditions.

11

After lunch, we headed back up to the fortress. With more time on our hands, we wandered around the stockpile of military machinery we'd somehow missed the night before. Cannons, tanks, machine guns, and missiles were everywhere, with only a few people looking at them. Afterwards, Michael insisted we visit the fortress museum. It was located inside one of the tower entrances.

After paying the cheap fee, we entered the thankfully small museum, where a young woman quickly offered her service as a guide.

"Giving tour in English is good practice for me," she said. "It is not often I do this. But I can speak German, Russian, or Italian if you wish? And Serbian, of course."

We followed the woman, who told us she was a student at the University of Belgrade, into a rectangular room with three displays set in the centre. Around the edge of the room were headless statues that looked Roman or perhaps Greek. The guide led us to the central displays. Each one contained a small-scale model of how the fortress had changed over time.

"The Turks destroyed much of the fortress in the sixteenth century," she told us, pointing at one of the mock-ups. The model didn't show any battle damage. Instead, it looked normal and fortress-like. "But eventually the Austrians came and rebuilt it."

We walked to another model and saw that the Austrians had done a good job. "Come," the woman said. "I show you some pottery."

I knew it, I thought. Every museum had to have a section dedicated to pottery, and to me, there was nothing duller than staring at an old clay bowl or an ancient ceramic plate. We both followed the guide to the pots in question, and while she droned on about them, my mind wandered, as it did every time.

I'd accepted long ago that I was a museum heathen, despite my best efforts to counter this. I simply couldn't bring myself to enjoy the pleasures of terracotta stoneware, even if it did date from a million years ago.

"And this is a Turkish cannon," she told us a few moments later. My mind refocused, and I regarded the thing. It was next to the pots, but had wooden wheels, a small metal cylinder, and a placard that read: *8cm Turkish Muzzle-Loading Cannon*. "It is how the Turks took Belgrade. They had this sort of firepower, and no one else did."

After a quick look at some muskets and long daggers, we thanked the guide and left. It was time for a coffee.

12

"So what do you think of Belgrade?" I asked Michael, as we sat in a busy outdoor cafe in the centre of the city. We were shaded from the sun under a large cream-coloured parasol emblazoned with Jelen Pivo. Glass-fronted buildings advertising the latest digital cameras surrounded us, and the locals of Belgrade were passing by with a parade of shopping bags and ice creams.

"I like it," Michael said, absently looking over at a couple of dark-skinned teenage boys. One had a violin, and the other was tinkling on an accordion. Their tune wafted over us as our coffees arrived. "I like it because of its history, and I like it because it's off the beaten track. And I like it because it's so cheap!"

Both of us watched the musicians for a moment. An elderly man wearing a blue cap approached them. He stood to one side, watching and listening. Then, without saying anything, he rummaged in his pockets and deposited some coins into the open violin case. Both boys bowed graciously, and the man walked off.

"Have you heard of Tesla?" asked Michael.

Surprisingly I had. I'd owned a 1980s rock album by an American band called Tesla. They'd called their album *The Great Radio Controversy*. I told Michael this. He was impressed.

"Yeah, but Tesla was actually a mad inventor. Have you heard of the Tesla Coil?"

I shook my head.

"Well there's a museum not far from here dedicated to him. If we find it, I'm pretty sure it will have one in it. You'll like it. I promise."

I sighed. "Another museum? We've already done one today. You know what I think about museums."

"I know. But this one doesn't have pots or jugs in it. It'll be fun...it'll be electric!"

I sighed again, this time more deeply. "You owe me a beer for this."

13

Nikola Tesla was born in Serbia in 1856. Best known for his work in the fields of magnetism and electricity, it was also rumoured that he was born during a lightning storm. Whether this was true or not, the man certainly liked electricity.

After a stint working in Budapest as an electrician, young Tesla boarded a ship bound for New York. The year was 1884, and Tesla was twenty-eight. During the trip, thieves stole his money, his ticket and most of his belongings. He wasn't the only one to fall foul of the thieves, and soon a mutiny broke out aboard the ship. At one point, Tesla was almost thrown overboard, but he managed to escape. He eventually arrived in America, with four cents in his wallet, and a letter of recommendation from his old employer.

Thanks to the letter, Thomas Edison hired Nikola Tesla as an electrical engineer in his company. At first, the new recruit was given simple electrical problems to solve, but when he proved himself exceptionally skilled, Edison promoted the Serb to higher office. Soon Tesla was putting his mind to some of the hardest and most perplexing jobs in the company. He solved them all with aplomb. But then both men fell out, and Tesla decided to strike out on his own.

Nikola Tesla did well as his own boss, inventing a whole catalogue of electrical gizmos (including early forms of fluorescent light bulbs and X-ray machines), which made him a fairly rich man. In 1891, he began his famous research into radio, but a costly patent battle with Guglielmo Marconi ended up thwarting Tesla. The upshot was that the Italian became famous as the Father of Radio, and Tesla became bitter. In this depression, Tesla came up with his strangest idea ever.

His directed-energy weapon could, he claimed, destroy anything in its path, including fleets of enemy aircraft. Not surprisingly, the press dubbed it the *death ray*. While negotiations were going on for the production rights, Tesla became suspicious, thinking spies were trying to steal his ideas.

As his paranoia increased, the inventor's behaviour turned more bizarre. For instance, after taking up permanent residence in a New York hotel, he began to abhor any form of jewellery, and he started to detest circular objects. He couldn't bring himself to touch hair, and made sure that anyone who cleaned his cutlery did so with exactly 18 napkins. He also distrusted overweight people, and thought that people who wore strange clothes were his enemy. But he did like pigeons.

Every day, for the final few years of his life, Tesla visited a nearby park to feed them. When he found an injured white pigeon one day, he took it to his hotel. There he made a special device that supported the pigeon's broken wing and leg, enabling it to heal. When the female pigeon was back to full health, Tesla took it back to the park and let it go. But every time he returned, the white pigeon would fly to him. He claimed that he loved that particular pigeon 'as a man loves a woman.'

Tesla died in January 1943, aged 86, leaving behind heavy debts. And in the end, his death ray never materialised. All his belongings were put into storage, and his body cremated. In 1952, Tesla's estate was shipped to Belgrade. A few years later, his ashes were sent over too. They currently reside inside a gold-plated sphere within the Nikola Tesla Museum.

14

The museum was quite small, taking up only a few rooms, one of which contained some of the great man's personal belongings. Another displayed the golden urn with his ashes inside. One section of the museum had a screen and some chairs. Three people were already sitting there, watching a movie about Tesla's life. Michael and I joined them, nodding at the others as we did so.

The movie was showing some black-and-white photos of Tesla's laboratory, and then of some scary-looking electrical bolts shooting out of strange contraptions. But then my mind began to wander as the narrator explained about how things worked. I looked at the other people in the room. There was a young couple and an older man, who looked like an inventor himself, due to his shock of unkempt hair. Everyone, apart from me, was transfixed by the screen, now showing a photo of Tesla. His dark hair and thick moustache made him look like a silent movie star. Suddenly the room erupted into noise. Michael's bottle of water was clattering on the wooden floor, spinning wildly before coming to a stop near the woman's foot.

"Sorry," said Michael sheepishly, and perhaps even unnecessarily. After all, it was hardly the crime of the century. Then, with all eyes upon him, he said, "I was squeezing it too much."

He got up, retrieved the bottle, and left the small cinema in shame. I followed him out. When we'd moved a sufficient distance, I sniggered. Michael shot me a glance.

"Pure comedy," I said. "I can't believe you told them you were squeezing it. Why did you say that?"

"I don't know. It was a fairly inane thing to admit."

We headed off towards the Tesla Coil.

15

The strange contraption was in the centre of an adjoining room. It was about ten feet high, made of metal, and looked unimpressive. It was basically an upright copper cylinder with a bulbous ring at the top.

Behind the Tesla Coil was a poster of Tesla. In it, he was sitting underneath his coil whilst sparks of electricity danced around him. I looked back at the coil. It looked just about capable of making a loaf of bread.

A museum guide appeared, as did the three other people from the cinema room. Michael put his water bottle in his pocket. After telling us to gather around the coil, the guide dimmed the lights and then powered up the strange device.

As it crackled and hummed, I saw faint blue sparks coming from the top, and then, quite dramatically, it came to life with a loud and sudden bang. A long, blue arc of electricity sparked and fizzled, and it sounded like we were in some sort of electrical sub-station. Suddenly, a thick jagged line of electricity ran from the top of the cylinder to the sphere above. It looked like the sort of thing a ray gun would produce, all crackly and pure white. I was mesmerised, and so was everyone else. And then, without preamble, everything stopped. The lights came back on, and the Tesla Coil became still. With the show over, everyone clapped.

"Did you like it?" Michael asked as we headed outside.

I nodded. The Tesla Coil *had* been something worth seeing.

16

After lunch, Michael and I decided to walk to Saint Sava's Cathedral, named after a thirteenth-century Serbian Saint.

Saint Sava is Serbia's most venerated holy man, the patron saint of schoolchildren, no less. According to legend, his cathedral was built on the place where his remains were buried. But how they came to that particular spot makes for grim reading.

When Saint Sava died in 1236, his body was buried in southern Serbia. But then, almost 360 years after his death, something terrible happened. Someone dug him up.

This grisly deed occurred during the reign of the Ottoman Empire. A Serbian bishop named Teodor Nestorovic was leading an uprising against the Turks. His army of rebels carried flags with Saint Sava's image emblazoned on them as they went into battle. This angered the Turks, so the leader of the Ottoman forces ordered the exhumation of Sava's body. He wanted the Saint's remains brought to Belgrade so he could infuriate the Christian infidels.

Turkish troops rushed to the monastery where Saint Sava was buried, ordering monks to unearth the coffin. They did so under duress, and soon the Ottoman grave robbers were rushing back to Belgrade, slaughtering any monks who tried to hinder their progress. When they arrived in the capital, they carried the coffin up a hill. Then they built a pyre.

By now, the Serbs knew what was going on, which was exactly what the Ottomans wanted. With everyone watching, the Turks set fire to Sava's remains, and soon the flames could be seen across the Danube. With their saint and mascot burning, the rebels quickly weakened and fled to Transylvania. When the Turks caught up with Bishop Teodor Nestorovic, they flayed him alive.

17

The Cathedral of Saint Sava is huge. In fact, it is one of the largest churches in the world. And it looked superb; an all-white exterior topped with green domes and golden crosses. But what Michael and I couldn't believe was that it wasn't finished, even though construction had started in 1989.

We stepped into the vast interior. A few people stood with lit candles, staring at some icons, whilst others prayed by the entrance. Some sections of the cathedral looked nice and sparkly, such as the stained-glass windows and a few marble columns, but the presence of scaffolding and bare concrete spoiled the look.

"Why haven't they finished it?" I whispered to Michael as we walked around. The outside had been completed in 2009, but since then, nothing much had happened. We passed a portly man gazing upwards at the massive dome. I almost bumped into him.

"I'm not sure."

"The reason it is not finished," said the middle-aged and friendly-looking man we'd just passed, "is because it is the way things are done in Serbia. It takes time to get things right, and, anyway, there is no rush: Saint Sava's is not going anywhere. It will be done when it is done. Tell me something though; even though it is not finished, do you think this cathedral is still beautiful?"

Michael and I nodded, though a little tentatively.

The man nodded too, and gestured around at the cavernous area. "Saint Sava's is like Serbia itself. Beautiful but not complete. My country has gone through – and is going through – many changes. Our history is pitted with setbacks and misfortunes, but in the end, we will succeed. Serbia will be spectacular. Just like this cathedral."

We nodded again, trying to follow the logic of his argument. It was a strange metaphor to use, I thought, comparing the sloth-like fitting out of a cathedral with the history and politics of an actual nation. But I could see his point. Sort of.

The man smiled. "Well, have a good day in Belgrade." He walked off towards some ladies holding candles.

18

At precisely 8pm, on 24th March 1999, after peace talks had failed, NATO began airstrikes against Yugoslavia in an attempt to make Slobodan Milosevic's government end the civil war in Kosovo.

One thousand NATO aircraft began to fly missions across Yugoslavia (in particular Kosovo), taking out strategic military targets. Sometimes they sent missiles into Serbia. On 7th May, while trying to hit specific targets in downtown Belgrade, NATO cruise missiles smashed into the Chinese Embassy, killing three Chinese journalists. NATO apologised, saying they thought the building had been a military warehouse.

Many missiles did hit the right target though, and by June 1999, Milosevic agreed to withdraw troops from Kosovo.

Some of the wounds from these airstrikes are still visible in Belgrade today. Michael and I found one such building, formerly the Yugoslavian Army Headquarters. It was in the centre of the city.

It looked like an earthquake had struck it. Collapsed floors, missing windows, bent girders, and sections with no roof lent an air of war to it. Why it had been left to rot we had no idea, but as a stark reminder of the conflict, it couldn't have been better placed. It was a truly remarkable sight in an otherwise unremarkable part of the city.

Michael shook his head. "I think they should level it."

Cars, lorries, taxis and trams were passing along the road, their passengers not even registering the eyesore any more. Pedestrians were the same, oblivious to the carnage, quite clearly used to seeing it every day of their lives. To them, it was invisible, or else simply part of the scenery.

"I disagree. I think they should leave it."

"...Why?"

"As a reminder."

19

"So that's Belgrade done," I said to Michael in a bar that evening. The weather was still warm and the bars full of people in good cheer. A nearby fountain erupted into a cascade of cooling spray. "And here's to Serbia."

We clinked glasses together: Jelen Pivo again.

Michael took a sip of his beer and said, "I've really enjoyed Belgrade. And getting you into two museums in one day is a personal best. I don't think I'll manage that feat again."

The sound of jet engines caught my attention. It was an airliner flying across the city to a destination unknown. It made me think about our next stop on the Odyssey, Sarajevo. Like Belgrade, the Bosnian capital had endured its fair share of misery and destruction. I was looking forward to getting there.

We finished our drinks and went to the hotel to pack.

2. Sarajevo, Bosnia & Herzegovina

Interesting fact: There are still unexploded mines in the hills of Sarajevo.

The JAT Airways turboprop from Belgrade to Sarajevo took only forty minutes, even if it did sound like a Lancaster bomber.

The first thing we did when we stepped into the arrivals hall of Sarajevo Airport was to change some British pounds into the local currency, the convertible mark. Then we caught a cheap taxi to our hotel.

From the taxi, we noticed how hilly Sarajevo was. It was on these hills that snipers hid during the Bosnian War. We also noticed the abundance of mosques. Minarets were everywhere, a distinct difference from the Orthodox Christianity of Serbia.

"Look," said Michael, pointing at a dilapidated building we were driving past. It was pockmarked with bullet holes.

The driver noticed us looking. "From war," he said.

2

The Siege of Sarajevo lasted for almost four years. It occurred between April 1992 and February 1996, making it the longest siege of a capital city in modern warfare.

Before the war, Muslim Bosnians (known as Bosniaks) made up 44% of Bosnia and Herzegovina's population. Bosnian Serbs and Bosnian Croats made up most of the remainder. When Yugoslavia started to fall apart, the Bosniaks held a referendum for independence. The Bosnian Serb population said they would boycott it. The Bosniaks didn't care and held it anyway. When the results in favour of independence came in, Bosnian Serbs began protesting.

Backed by Belgrade, Bosnian Serbs living in Serb-heavy regions of Bosnia began to assemble themselves into armed groups. They rounded up Bosniaks from their towns and villages and threw them out. Things escalated when Muslim settlements were ransacked or burnt to the ground. Then the killings began. One of the worst atrocities was the Srebrenica Massacre.

The massacre began with a Serb plan to capture all Bosniak men of fighting age in the town of Srebrenica. But in the round up, young boys and older men were taken too. Serb militia trucked the Bosniaks to abandoned schools and warehouses, holding the men there before driving them to execution fields. In groups, the men were lined up and shot. Then the next busload arrived. It was an effective but slow process. To speed things up, instead of bussing the Bosniaks to the fields, the Serbs simply tossed hand grenades into the warehouses.

Eleven days later, more than eight thousand Bosnian Muslims were dead. The man in charge of the death squads was Ratko Mladic, later described as the Butcher of Bosnia. In 2012, Mladic's trial opened in The Hague. The former military commander was accused of war crimes and genocide. The United Nations described the massacre as the worst crime on European soil since the Second World War.

"Here is your hotel," said the taxi driver, pulling up next to a large yellow building. During some of the worst periods of the siege, foreign journalists had stayed in the Holiday Inn. It was situated along the infamous Sniper Alley, and was hit a fair few times, suffering widespread damage. This gave the hotel the distinction of offering its most attractive rooms below ground level.

We paid the taxi driver and stood in Sniper Alley.

3

During the Bosnian War, *Ulica Zmaja od Bosne* was the main thoroughfare of Sarajevo. It still is. Lined with tall buildings and hills on either side, snipers had plenty of places to choose from. Signs saying *Pazi! Snajper* (*Watch out! Sniper*) became common along the road, but the civilians of Sarajevo sometimes had to get to the other side. Often they would simply run for it, or wait for UN armoured vehicles to cross, and then hide behind them. In the end though snipers killed 225 civilians, including 60 children.

Nowadays, the area around the Holiday Inn looks mundanely normal. There are no bullet holes, and no reminders of the war. The street was busy, with plenty of traffic plying the important route. The evening was warm, and the people waiting for buses and trams looked carefree and happy. Sniper Alley was just another busy street in another European city.

As Michael and I walked into the foyer of the Holiday Inn, a few words sprung to mind: opulence and grandeur were just two of them. There was a huge lampshade dangling from the high ceiling, and luxurious seating for anyone wanting a drink.

The hotel was sometimes popular with movie stars, due to the Sarajevo Film Festival held every August. Famous people like Bono, John Malkovich, Kevin Spacey and many more had visited the festival in the past, and possibly even walked across the carpet that Michael and I were now crossing. The Sarajevo Film Festival was actually the biggest of its kind in the Balkans, and had begun its life in 1995, during the siege of Sarajevo. Even in the midst of aerial bombardment, fifteen thousand people somehow managed to see the films.

4

Venturing out into the Sarajevo night, we went to find a bar. Five minutes later, we came across one, and walked up to the door. Some pretty girls were guarding the entrance. "Hi!" they said smiling. "Are you on the guest list?"

Yes, I'm Brad Pit, and this is Tom Cruise is what we should have said, but instead I shook my head. "No, I'm afraid we're not."

"Then I'm sorry. You can't come in. This is a private party."

We walked on, and eventually came across another bar that allowed us entry. We sat outside on some high stools and ordered some beers.

"We couldn't have done this fifteen years ago," I said to Michael. "Sat here and enjoyed a beer."

"No," he agreed, taking a slurp of his Sarajevsko. His slight grimace gave away the fact that he wasn't really a beer or lager drinker. Michael's favourite tipples were alcopops or cider, but with a distinct lack of them for sale across Belgrade and Sarajevo, he'd been forced to settle for lager. "Not unless we wanted a sniper to set us in his sights."

The other people in the bar looked like locals, all of them enjoying a summer's night out. They were all in their twenties, and I wondered whether any of them had been in Sarajevo during the siege. If so, they had been small children.

During the siege, one and half thousand children lost their lives, most killed by mortar attacks. A report by UNICEF compiled after the war stated that half of Sarajevo's children had seen someone being shot, and 39% had witnessed a family member being killed. Perhaps the most depressing statistic of all, though, was that 40% of children in the city had been directly shot at themselves.

I knew that the Balkan Wars boiled down to the range of ethnic groups in the former Yugoslavia, but couldn't recall what had actually kicked off the whole thing. Michael was bound to know, however. He'd done a lot of reading in preparation for our trip. I asked him what had happened.

5

"Things began to bubble when Tito died in the early '80s," Michael told me. "Before that, all the Yugoslav republics had a bit of freedom to run their own affairs. But the thing is, they all knew Tito was in charge, and that he'd come down hard if they messed around. Most people were happy with this arrangement, apart from Kosovo."

"Why Kosovo?"

"Because it wasn't classed as an actual republic; it was just a province of Serbia. Most people in Kosovo were ethnic Albanians and therefore Muslim. They were angry that they were not allowed to run their own affairs - like the other Yugoslav republics could. They had to abide by rules from Belgrade."

Michael took another drink and continued. "Think about the UK. There's England, Scotland, Wales and Northern Ireland. All of them sort out their own affairs, but they know that London is in overall control. Agree?"

"Yeah."

"So imagine if a part of England - let's say a made-up region of Northshire - decides this isn't fair. Northshire has its own language, its own history, and its people are ethnically different. It even has its own religion. So why can't it be like Wales or Scotland? It's not as if Northshire wants to leave the United Kingdom or anything. No, all it wants is the same degree of freedom as the others."

"Sound fair enough to me," I said.

"Exactly. But London won't allow it. And that's more or less what it was like in Yugoslavia for the people of Kosovo."

Michael told me that by the late eighties, Yugoslavia was in economic trouble. A fifth of its workforce was unemployed, mainly in Bosnia and Herzegovina, Macedonia, Kosovo and Serbia itself.

"Croatia and Slovenia weren't as badly affected. They were doing okay, and even reckoned they were propping up the poorer republics. This was another bone of contention within Yugoslavia. They thought the politicians in Belgrade were making a mess of everything. Eventually, both of them decided they wanted looser ties with Serbia. That's what kick-started the war. Belgrade didn't want to give them any freedom."

6

The next morning, we jumped in a taxi and drove to the Tunnel Museum. Along the highway, I noticed a road sign saying 'Tuzla', a place made famous during the Bosnian Conflict. On 25th May 1995, Serb forces had fired a shell into a busy street there, killing 71 civilians, including a two-year-old child.

Mind you, a few years prior to that atrocity, Muslim forces had killed 109 Serbs in the village of Bjelovac. And in the village of Kravica, Bosniak forces had attacked property and people, killing another 49 Bosnian Serbs. Both sides were not wholly innocent in the war that had swept the region.

The taxi headed westwards along Sniper Alley, and then began a series of turns into the foothills near the airport. Some buildings still showed signs of war, blemished with visible bullet holes. A few minutes later, we arrived at our destination.

The Tunnel Museum was a small, two-storey house with its lower floor dedicated to the famous tunnel. Bullet holes covered the front of the building. The house itself was located in the middle of a rural road, complete with an untethered goat munching on some bushes.

During the Siege of Sarajevo, someone in the Bosniak army decided a tunnel was needed. Construction began underneath the house Michael and I were looking at. It stretched for 800m, until it surfaced at the other side of the airport, which was under United Nations control. As well as soldiers and weapons coming through the tunnel, food and aid made its way along. And citizens could escape too. The tunnel soon established itself as a lifeline to Bosniaks trapped in Sarajevo.

We walked through the entrance, and discovered we were the only visitors. A kindly man introduced himself and led us to a small side room where we watched a short DVD about the conflict. One scene showed a shell hitting the Holiday Inn. It also told us that the tunnel had taken four months to build, constructed by shovel-wielding soldiers. Their daily payment was one packet of cigarettes, a much sought-after commodity in siege-stricken Sarajevo.

After the video, the man led us around some of the museum's exhibits, including some uniforms and flags. "Now I show you tunnel," he said.

7

The entrance to the tunnel was down some wooden steps. The man told us to go by ourselves. We thanked him and climbed down. Michael and I walked along the tunnel's length (just twenty metres now), seeing for ourselves things previously seen on the video. Both of us had to crouch low to make our way through, negotiating the narrow rails at the bottom, our hands providing balance on the wooden beams running along the sides.

The tunnel was lit by a few strategically placed bulbs, and the only sound was our feet upon the boards. Because of the poor drainage inside the tunnel, it often flooded, with water sloshing around people's waists. I tried to imagine hundreds of people trudging through, with railway carts, an oil pipe and electrical cables hindering their passage. Outside, shells might have been booming. And they could have been in the tunnel for two hours. It must have been terrifying.

A few minutes later, Michael and I came out the other end, ascending some more wooden steps leading to sunlight. We seemed to be in the middle of a farmer's field, with bright yellow melons littering the ground. In the distance was the airport.

"I didn't expect that to be so moving," I told Michael, as we stared about our surroundings. Being inside the tunnel had been a strangely humbling experience for me, and I didn't really know why. Michael nodded thoughtfully, but said nothing.

Suddenly a small cat appeared, and then stopped when it noticed us. After turning tail, it ran back into the melon field. We headed for a small room filled with photos and newspaper cuttings.

Children of Sarajevo Slaughtered by Serbs, one dark headline read. Published by The Independent on 26th June 1995, it made for grim reading.

That evening, a group of children had been enjoying themselves in a local playground. Without warning, a shell exploded near them. It killed three of the children and two adults. On that same day, in another part of town, a shell hit a market place. It killed two little girls, their bodies ripped apart in the blast.

"Let's get out of here," I said. "This is harrowing."

8

The taxi dropped us off in the old town of Sarajevo, in a square known as Bascarsija. One side was made up of small shops, but mainly Bascarsija was outdoor cafes and pigeons. Hundreds of them had gathered near a large tree, where a few people stood feeding them. In the centre of the square was a Turkish fountain.

The fountain didn't look like a fountain in the traditional sense: it was more of a wooden building with a domed green roof. Its base was made of stone, and some taps offered water to the people of Sarajevo. Pigeons roosted on the roof.

The Turks had founded Sarajevo in the 15th century, and, at its peak, a hundred years later, it became one of the most important Ottoman towns in the Balkans, second only to Istanbul. But then fire and warfare destroyed it, and, by the time the Austrians arrived, only the central old town remained.

Michael and I sat in one of the cafes along the square's edge, protected from the sun by a red Coca-Cola parasol. I remarked to Michael how we could be sitting in a Middle Eastern city, not a European one. In fact, it was how I imagined Beirut, or maybe Amman to be. Women in Muslim veils wandered past (though there were still plenty of women favouring Western clothing), and tantalising smoke floated from kebab stalls. Along one nearby street, we could see shops peddling copper goods, jewellery, and pottery. The endless minarets in the hills cemented the illusion. It all seemed so exotic.

"I've been thinking about the Tunnel Museum," said Michael a short while later. I looked at him. He looked pensive. "To me, it had an edge of propaganda about it."

"Propaganda?"

"Yeah. It only gave the Bosnian Muslim side of the story."

I scoffed. "But they were the ones being mortared by the Serbs! Dozens of them were dying every day. And the tunnel provided medicine and supplies. It was a lifeline. I don't understand what you mean by propaganda?"

"Yes, they were under siege, no one disputes that. But think about it. Why didn't more civilians escape through the tunnel?"

I thought many had; I told Michael this.

"Yes, but only a tiny minority. From what I know, the Bosniak authorities placed a heavy restriction on the people leaving through the tunnel. Plus, anyone who wanted to go through it had to obtain written permission from an office in the centre of Sarajevo. And you know what that meant. So they didn't exactly make it easy for people, did they? And get this: some people had to pay to enter the tunnel."

I was taken aback by the last statement. "Really?"

"Yeah, really." Michael flicked a fly from his arm. "Look, the tunnel did bring aid into the city, and it also allowed *some* people to get out, but it was also a good tool to highlight the plight of the Bosnian people. Look at it this way: if everyone had escaped through it, then there wouldn't have been any UN air strikes, and maybe Serb troops would have taken over Sarajevo. And now we would be sitting in a bar in Serbia."

I thought about this for a moment. "The tunnel saved lives, not destroyed them."

Michael sat back in his chair. "I know. But it's just something to think about, isn't it?"

9

After lunch, while we were still sitting in the square, a beggar approached. He wasn't the first beggar we'd encountered in the Bosnian capital. Earlier that day, before we'd gone to the Tunnel Museum, Michael had bought himself a bag of plums from a shop, and, as we walked back to the hotel, a young street urchin, most probably Roma, began hassling him for some. When Michael ignored him, the boy made a quick grab for the bag, but failed. He quickly scarpered.

This beggar was older, maybe in his early twenties. He had a few missing teeth and a piece of paper in his hand. What it said, neither of us had any idea, because it was written in Cyrillic. The man said nothing. I turned to him and shook my head. He nodded and wandered off to some women at the next table. They read his note and gave him a few marks. Ten minutes later, another beggar approached. This one was a boy aged about five.

He looked healthy enough, but his outstretched hand gave us the unmistakable gesture of want. Again I shook my head, but this boy wasn't about to give up so easily. Leaning over the table, he stretched his hand even closer, giving us a large smile. His teeth looked in good shape, I noticed, meaning he was getting decent food from somewhere. Fishing around in my pocket, I plucked out a half mark coin, and tossed it to the boy. He grabbed it, uttering something in Bosnian, and was off, bothering the people at the next table.

And then something interesting happened. As I looked over at the fountain, I saw another boy, aged about ten, stoop down and collect something from the ground. I assumed it was a coin. I was about to turn away when he threw the object at a woman sitting at the edge of our café. The stone smashed near the woman's foot, causing her to jump in shock. As she flustered around, the boy was already searching for a new missile, and I wondered whether it would be prudent to move tables. If the boy misjudged his next shot, we would be in the line of fire.

As the boy scoured the ground, the woman came out of her stupor and rushed over to him. Pigeons scattered in all directions, but she managed to grab him by a skinny arm, and shook him like a rag doll. She was yelling and cursing, but the boy simply laughed. This made the woman angrier, causing people to point and stare.

Knowing she could do nothing, she let the boy go, and marched off towards her seat, fury etched on her face. The boy shouted something at the woman, and then wandered off with a nonchalant air about him.

"My God!" I said to Michael, finally taking a sip of Sarajevsko. "This is better than TV." But the fun wasn't over. Michael spotted a stooped ancient man and pointed him out. He had no teeth and must have been at least ninety. He loitered at the edge of the cafe, wobbling slightly until a waitress approached. She leaned in close while he said something, and then, after regarding him for a moment, she nodded. The man produced a small bag from his pocket and emptied it on a table. It was a pile of coins. The woman counted them, and disappeared into the cafe. She returned a few moments later and handed him a couple of banknotes. These he clutched as if he couldn't believe they were actually in his possession.

"I love Sarajevo," I said to Michael. "In fact, it might be the best place I've ever been. It's so different from what I expected, so colourful, so full of life. Belgrade doesn't even compare."

10

Imagine being nineteen years old, waiting in ambush, armed with a pistol and a cyanide pill. Also imagine, though it would be almost impossible to do so, that your actions would later alter the course of history. Well, a young man called Gavrilo Princip was doing exactly that in Sarajevo. He was a Bosnian Serb.

Early in the morning of 28th June 1914, a group of six young men, including Princip, had spread themselves out along the Miljacka River. Between them they had six bombs, four revolvers and a collection of cyanide pills. They were lying in wait for Archduke Franz Ferdinand, heir to the Austria-Hungary throne, who was going to be travelling through the streets of Sarajevo with his wife, Sophie.

As the gang lurked in the shadows, hundreds of well-wishers came and lined the streets, waiting to wave at the Austrian visitors. Princip and his pals prepared themselves. At 10am, the Archduke's motorcade, consisting of seven cars (Ferdinand's was the third), set off from a nearby army camp. Near the river, one of Princip's co-conspirators hid in front of a cafe. This particular gang member was going to be first in line as the motorcade passed. As crowds of well-wishers began to wave and cheer, the man knew the Archduke's car was about to pass, but lost his nerve. He later claimed a police officer had been standing nearby. No matter: five assassins remained.

The second man failed in his task too. The reason he later gave was that he'd given his bomb and gun to a fellow plotter. Still four conspirators remained. That should be enough, surely.

Unaware of the terrible interest in them, the Archduke and his wife blithely continued their journey along the river in their open-topped car, heading towards man number three. This assassin was hiding in an alleyway, and, as Ferdinand's car drew near, the young man held his nerve and threw his bomb. Whether it bounced off the Archduke's car and rolled under the wheels of the car behind, or whether the driver of Ferdinand's car spotted the assassination attempt and sped up, no one really knows. Either way, the bomb destroyed the fourth car of the cavalcade, wounding the occupants as well as some people in the crowd.

The bomber promptly swallowed his cyanide pill and jumped in the river. But the stretch of water he chose was only four inches deep, and worse, his pill failed to work. An angry crowd dragged him out and started beating him. When the police arrived, they dispersed the mob and arrested the man.

Understandably, the scene in downtown Sarajevo turned to chaos. The car containing Ferdinand sped off towards the Town Hall, making it impossible for the remaining assassins to get a clear shot. As the Archduke raced past, he shouted at the crowd, 'So you welcome your guests with bombs?' The assassins had no choice but to disband.

After recovering in the Town Hall, Franz Ferdinand and his wife decided to visit the hospital to see some of the wounded. This decision proved pivotal. Gavrilo Princip had just come out of a local food store, just off the Latin Bridge, the most famous bridge in Sarajevo, when, with horrendous timing, the Archduke's car started reversing along the same street. When Princip realised who it was, he couldn't believe his luck, especially when the Archduke's driver stalled the engine.

The nineteen-year-old assassin pulled out his gun and fired twice. One bullet hit the Archduke in the neck; the other entered Sophie's abdomen. As the car sped off again, both victims remained upright. "Sophie dear, don't die. Stay alive for our children," were Ferdinand's last words before they both died.

Back near the bridge, a crowd gathered around Princip. He took his cyanide pill, but like the other one, it failed to work. In desperation, he tried to shoot himself, but a man wrestled the gun from his grasp. After a good beating from the mob, he was placed into custody, and the repercussions of his actions reverberated throughout Europe, giving the spark to ignite the First World War.

As well as Princip, all the conspirators were captured and then tried. Those aged over twenty were executed by hanging; the others received prison sentences averaging 15 years. Many of the men died of tuberculosis after only a few years of incarceration, with Princip himself succumbing to the disease after just four years. Incredibly, two of the plotters were released from prison in 1918, when the Allies defeated Germany. One of them, a man called Vaso Cubrilovic, became a teacher in Sarajevo, and then a professor at the University of Belgrade. He died in 1990, aged 93.

11

Michael and I walked over the historic pedestrian-only Latin Bridge, now an icon of Sarajevo. The arched stone crossing, supported by three sturdy columns, was the oldest bridge in Sarajevo, and dated from Ottoman times.

We stopped in the middle to stare out over the river. It wasn't particularly wide, or fast-flowing, but it had surged enough times to damage the bridge.

Stone walls marked the riverbank, giving it a canal-like appearance, and the buildings beyond looked grand, but faded from their best. A large cement truck trundled along the road, causing vibrations on the bridge. Up in the hills, the city's mosques had just sprung into action, giving the call to prayer for its Muslim citizens. It was hard to believe such a world-changing event had happened so close to where we were standing. Only a plaque on a nearby wall told the story of that day.

"It says here," said Michael, reading from his guidebook, "that there's an old Ottoman Inn called Morica Han. In the middle ages, herders and tradesmen from the East used to stay there with their animals. Do you fancy having a look?"

"Is it a museum?"

"No, I think it's a cafe or something."

"Okay."

Ten minutes later, we found the old inn. Inside the entrance was a fabric market selling Persian carpets, and just beyond that was a large courtyard filled with tables and chairs. It seemed popular with the people of Sarajevo, so we decided to sit down and order something. While we waited for some menus, Michael pointed a few things out to me.

"Upstairs was where the people stayed," he told me, pointing at the second level of the courtyard. Large shuttered windows looked down over the restaurant. "It could hold about three hundred people. And down here was where the animals were kept. Up to seventy horses."

When the waitress arrived, I decided to order a Bosnian Coffee for 1 Mark (40p), which arrived on a copper plate. Michal ordered some traditional lemonade that came with a couple of sugar lumps.

"What do I do with this?" I asked Michael, prodding the cube of Turkish Delight that came with my drink. I had a couple of sugar cubes as well.

Michael shrugged. "Why don't you put it in the coffee? It might melt it. Put the sugar in too."

I picked up the small cup of hot brown liquid to have a taste first. If it was okay, I would not be adding anything; however, the taste of the coffee was far too strong and acidic for my liking. So, taking Michael's advice, I added everything to the mix, stirring it, in the hope of melting the Turkish Delight. It didn't want to melt, though, and so I left it a while until it seemed softer. Then I took a tentative sip.

"Well?" asked Michael.

"Not bad." It was actually rather nice. And when I'd finished, I slugged back the by now soft Turkish Delight and ate it as well. I was happy with my first Bosnian Coffee, even though I'd done it completely wrong.

Later I found out that the process for drinking a Bosnian Coffee was to dip one of the sugar cubes into the coffee and then bite it in half. With the section of the sugar cube held tightly between the teeth, I should've taken a sip of the coffee, the sugar adding sweetness as the coffee passed through it. The Turkish delight was simply there as a side dish to accompany the coffee.

12

At around lunchtime on 5th February 1994, a mortar shell landed in the centre of the open-air Markale Market. The market was busy at the time, with shoppers and stall holders crowding the tightly packed aisles. The shell exploded, killing 68 people and wounding 144 more. A lake of blood covered the floor. Crumpled, broken torsos, severed limbs, and crushed body parts gave the place the appearance of a nightmare. News stories across the world showed footage of the massacre, and I could recall watching some of it myself.

Eighteen months later, on 28th August 1995, a second massacre occurred when Serbs fired five shells at the same market. This time they killed 37 people. This event was the turning point in the Siege of Sarajevo. NATO decided it could no longer stand back. Two days later, air strikes against Serb forces were staged, quickly putting an end to the siege. Sarajevo opened its roads and borders to the outside world.

Michael and I walked into the open-air Markale Market and saw nothing to indicate the horror that had occurred in the 1990s. Today, it just looked like any other fruit and vegetable market. Men and women sat among mounds of peppers, grapes, bananas and tomatoes, occasionally weighing them in antique scales. It had been just like this when the mortars came, I thought sadly, with people wandering about trying to bag a bargain. Towards the rear of the market was a large maroon panel with a list of names written on it: the victims of both Markale Massacres.

13

Only later did we find out that rabid dogs roamed the hills around Sarajevo. And, even worse, unexploded landmines still dotted the fields. The afternoon was hot, and soon Michael and I were panting like rabid dogs ourselves.

"Are you sure we're going the right way?" I said, without keeling over. Perhaps that earlier pint of beer had been a bad idea. I felt lightheaded and drowsy. We were on a steep incline, passing a few houses and shops, one of which sold only wooden brooms and brushes.

"Yeah," panted Michael. "The White Garrison is up here, trust me."

The White Garrison was an old fortification located high up in Vratnik Hills. It supposedly offered amazing views, which was why we were climbing up to it. A woman in a headscarf passed us on the way down the hill. She was carrying two large bags of vegetables. In some nearby fields, men were busy with hoes, and, further up, we passed a group of squawking children playing football in a walled alleyway.

We came to a large cemetery filled with thin white gravestones. Each one was set in a well-manicured plot, spread out across a sea of green grass. One of the gravestones read: *Kenan Kuric, 1958-1995*. He'd died during the siege of Sarajevo aged 37.

Every gravestone had Islamic lettering etched on them, and all had a similar year of death. This was a graveyard for Bosnian Muslims killed during the siege. The cemetery covered an entire terrace of the hill. It overlooked the terracotta roofs of the city below. We passed through it in silence.

Michael paused ahead of me, looking this way and that. Some high buildings on both sides of the track obscured his view. He looked red and seemed lost. When I caught up with him, he finally admitted that we might have taken a wrong turn.

"Bloody hell, Michael!" I croaked. My tongue was sticking to my mouth, and I could hardly breathe. "How much of a wrong turn?"

"Not sure."

Michael's bald patch was glinting under the sun's rays, and had already turned an unpleasant red colour. I turned to look at a group of small boys who had been watching our passage with interest.

All five were sitting on a wall with a football by their feet. I waved at them, but none waved back. Instead they preferred to giggle and stare at the stupid Englishmen walking up a mountain in the heat of the midday sun.

I went up to the boys, all aged about eight, and showed them the guidebook. It had the name of the White Garrison printed in Bosnian as well as in English. The boys crowded around and then one boy nodded, gesturing for me to follow. He walked past Michael, and after fifty yards or so, he stopped and pointed. In front of him were some steep stone steps.

"You go...there!" he said in broken English, sweeping his arm in the direction of the steps. I looked at the gradient and prayed he was telling the truth. I handed him a couple of marks, and he ran off.

Michael and I took to the steps, climbing ever upwards, until we came to an area of hills. With a snaking path, we decided to take a shortcut, and crossed over grassland, and bounded over walls. Somehow we managed to evade the landmines. Eventually, after what seemed an eternity, we reached a summit, and then, like a mirage, a bar appeared. I headed straight for it while Michael stopped to take some photos.

Ordering some drinks, I got chatting to the barman. He told me the bar was popular with German tourists. "Wait," he suddenly said, and hurried off. As I took a deep gulp of my beer, some distinctive German Beer Hall music started up. It was all brass instruments and deep male vocals. Michael arrived in the bar and looked at me quizzically. We were the only people there, and the music was almost deafening.

The man appeared again with a large grin on his face. "Good, yah?" he shouted, swivelling his head around to regard the speaker system. I smiled and nodded as he disappeared behind the bar.

Michael sat down. "What's going on?" he shouted above the melee.

"I'm not sure."

"Why the German music?"

I shrugged. "He must think we're German."

The White Garrison turned out to be disappointing after the trek we'd endured to reach it. Just a pile of ruins really. But the views were spectacular. We could see right down the valley as well as into the surrounding hillsides. A prime spot for snipers, no doubt.

14

As evening fell over Sarajevo, and the lights came on, we realised there was only one more thing we wanted to see - a famous Sarajevo Rose.

Sarajevo Roses were scattered all around the city, and we found two of them on Tita Street, lying innocuously on the pavement. The citizens of Sarajevo were being careful to walk around them because of what they represented.

During the Siege of Sarajevo, 300 hundred mortar shells a day had hit the streets and buildings of the city, killing many people in the process. Each mortar had left a floral-looking fragmentation pattern in the pavement as it hit. The patterns supposedly resembled flowers, perhaps roses.

The Sarajevo Roses on Tita Street were red. Their indentations had been filled with red resin to signify that people had died in the attack. By looking at the direction of the 'petals', we could see the approximate path the shells had come from - up in the hills. These Sarajevo Roses, like others in the city, were a fitting testament to those who had lost their lives during the siege.

How long the Sarajevo Roses would last though was unclear. As Sarajevo's streets underwent repairs, and its pavements were overhauled, the red roses were slowly disappearing. Whether any would survive the next decade was anyone's guess.

"So sad," I remarked, staring down at the red pattern. We headed back to the main square to find a bar.

15

"So, tomorrow we have to be up early for our flight," I said.

Michael nodded. Our 6.30am departure would mean getting up at about 4am, something neither of us were looking forward to. After changing planes in Belgrade, we would then head onwards to Pula in Croatia. Not that we'd see much of the old Roman city; we would be heading up the coast to the town of Porec (pronounced Porr-ech) more or less immediately.

"So what did you think of Sarajevo?" I asked Michael. He already knew it was in my top five cities visited.

"I preferred Belgrade."

I was taken aback. "Really?"

"Yeah. Don't get me wrong, I enjoyed Sarajevo, but I don't know why you like it so much. Belgrade is just...a bit more interesting. A bit more...I don't know...more lively, I suppose."

"You're joking?"

Michael shook his head.

To me, there was no contest. Belgrade was just another European city, whereas Sarajevo was something entirely different. Perhaps it was to do with the siege, or maybe it was to do with the juxtaposition of mosques and churches, I didn't know, but Sarajevo seemed more *alive* than Belgrade.

A few hours later, after a meaty meal and a few more beers, we headed back to the Holiday Inn to pack. Croatia was the next country on the Odyssey.

3. Porec, Croatia

Interesting fact: The largest truffle in the world was found in Croatia.

"Did you know," said the man opposite us, a bushy-moustached individual in his late thirties, "that the fountain pen was invented in Croatia?" His accent suggested he was a local man.

We were sitting on a bus that was taking us up the coast to Porec, a journey that would take around one hour. From the airport, we'd caught a quick taxi to Pula Bus Station before boarding the northbound bus. The man talking to us had joined us a few stops later.

I shook my head. As far as I was concerned, the only famous person from Croatia was Goran Ivanisevic, the former tennis champion. I looked at Michael to see what he thought of the fact. *I knew that already,* he mouthed to me.

"And Marco Polo was born in Croatia. I bet you didn't know that!" the man added. "He was born on the Croatian island of Korcula, but the Italians took him as theirs, because at the time, the island was under Venetian control."

"You should be a tour guide," I told him. The man's knowledge and spoken English were good.

"Me? A tour guide? I don't think so. Besides, I have a criminal record."

I glanced at Michael. I bet he didn't know that. Outside, I noticed, we were passing limestone crags dotted with slim cypress trees.

A criminal record? What sort of criminal record? And was it polite to ask for clarification? The three of us sat in silence, listening to the juddering of the bus's suspension.

"I think perhaps you wonder if I am a murderer, yes?" stated the man a minute later.

I didn't know what to say, and judging from Michael, nor did he. He was keeping his expression neutral and saying nothing. I decided to do the same thing.

"Well, I am not murderer," he said. "No, I have criminal record because I used to be thief. Many years ago, I stole cars, driving them into Albania. My car of choice was Volkswagen, but any German-made car would do. But that is all in past now. So that is why I cannot be tour guide."

2

Situated on the western edge of the Istrian peninsula, Porec is one of Croatia's more popular tourist destinations. Michael and I had decided to stay there for one simple reason. From Porec, it would be easy to visit Slovenia.

Because it was late by the time we arrived, we decided to have a few drinks in the hotel bar. We would save the sights of Porec for the next day. But the largely empty bar gave us a good opportunity to discuss how we should tackle the next stage of the Odyssey. After all, we had nothing booked from this point onwards, and everything would require careful planning.

Michael spread the large map of the Balkans out on our table, almost sending my bottle of Ozujsko lager toppling. I caught it just in time and tutted.

Both of us stared at the map. Porec was located at the far northwest of Croatia, and the Slovenian border was just north of it. "Bled or Ljubljana?" I asked, managing to say the Slovenian capital's name correctly. It was pronounced *Loo-blee-ah-nah*.

Michael pondered this. "If we've only got one day for Slovenia, I think we should go to Bled."

"I agree."

Bled was a town in the north of the tiny country, quite close to the Austrian border. It was famous for its lake and alpine scenery, and when we'd seen a picture of it on the Internet, we both agreed it would be a great place to visit. Ljubljana was reportedly pretty too, but with so little time available, we had to be selective in our choices.

"And then," I said, tracing my finger along the map, "we head down the Croatian coast to Dubrovnik. From there, we can hire a car for a few days, and maybe drive to Montenegro. After that, we need to get to Albania, but that is a problem for another day. What do you think?"

"We have a plan."

"Indeed we do."

Michael folded the map, and we picked up our drinks. The Balkan Odyssey was looking good.

3

On our first morning in Croatia, the weather was once again sunny. Michael and I took the pleasant fifteen-minute walk into Porec town, passing juicy fig trees and darting green coloured skinks. The Adriatic was to our left and with the town's harbour coming into view through the conifers, we were in fine spirits.

Ambling past markets selling the usual touristy fare, we passed the regal red and yellow Town Palace. As Michael looked up at the flags above the arches, a sudden movement on the steps grabbed my attention. I spotted another lizard. It was poking its head through a gap in one of the stone slabs. I tried to grab it, but the skink was too quick. With a flick of its tail, it was gone, darting back into the darkness.

The people on the street were a mixture of tourists and locals. A few ladies who belonged to the latter category were sporting dyed red hair and long floral dresses. Virtually every tourist, including us, favoured T-shirt and shorts. Visitors greatly outnumbered the locals of Porec.

Around a slight bend from the Town Palace was a small square. A Zagrebanka building, a few street cafes and a small casino made up most of the structures, but the most interesting thing was a large round fortification.

In ancient times, a stone wall had encircled Porec, but the Round Tower dated from the Venetian period. Instead of being a museum, it was actually a cafe and bar. We knew this because of the large banner wrapped around the top section: *Cafe-Bar*, it proudly proclaimed. We left it behind and headed past a small marina filled with pleasure craft and sun-seeking tourists, most of them German.

Croatia is not popular with British holidaymakers, because many Brits associate the country with war. Other nations are not so small-minded, however, particularly the Germans. They account for almost a quarter of the tourists in Croatia, closely followed by visitors from Slovenia, Italy and Austria. Less than 3% of people holidaying in Croatia are Brits. Michael and I were trailblazers.

4

The Croatian War of 1991-1995 was devastating for the country. Prior to the conflict, Croatia's coastline had been a popular summer holiday destination. For a period in the late 1980s, Yugoslavia's beaches had been busy with West Europeans wanting a cheap vacation.

The war destroyed a quarter of the economy and caused $27 billion of damage. Almost 180,000 homes were destroyed, thousands of heritage sites were blown up or damaged, and millions of landmines were laid. It took until 2009 before the Croatian authorities had marked the positions of these mines, but not before they had killed 500 people.

During the conflict, Serb forces attacked numerous Croatian towns and cities, including the tourist hotspots of Dubrovnik and Split. Thousands of Croatian civilians and soldiers died, and thousands more went missing.

But Serbs suffered too. Croatian forces targeted Serb-heavy villages and towns during skirmishes. In 2013, there was fury following the conviction of two Croatian army commanders for war crimes against Serbs. To Croats, the Generals were heroes, but to the courts and Serbs, the men were criminals. Evidence given at their trials showed that the generals had ordered the shelling of homes in southwest Croatia, knowing that Serb civilians were living in them.

Both countries still harbour deep grudges about the conflict.

5

Porec escaped the ravages of war. Its well-kept old town was set behind a protected harbour. Michael and I arrived at the main pedestrian thoroughfare, the cobbled Decumanus Street.

It was busy. Most people were browsing through the souvenirs on offer, or sampling the extensive range of ice creams for sale. Fat westerners waddled along the cobbles, clogging up a street already narrowed by street-side art galleries and men trying to sell sunglasses.

Be fair and I will bring peace to your city, was the quote inscribed at the top of another medieval structure, this one called the Pentagonal Tower. Like the Round Tower, it was about two storeys high, built by the Venetians in the fifteenth century, and had been there to fend off a possible Turkish attack. It also had a cafe inside. Michael and I climbed to the top, sat down, and ordered a coffee each.

"I think we should go to Slovenia tomorrow," I announced.

Michael stood up and walked to the ledge. "Yeah, good idea," he said. A minute later, he chuckled to himself. "A seagull has just crapped on a man's shoulder."

I joined Michael, and spotted the man straight away. He was looking at his shoulder while spinning around furiously, searching for the culprit. The bird was nowhere to be seen.

"How do you know it was a seagull?" I asked.

"I saw it. Amazing shot!"

We both sat down.

"About Slovenia," I said. "I think, to make it easy for ourselves, we should join an organised tour group. Daytrips to Bled are advertised everywhere. We pay the money, a coach picks us up, we see the castle, and come back. Simple and easy."

Michael pondered this. I knew what he was thinking. We were independent travellers, forging our own way forward into lands unknown. We didn't want to be tied to a schedule, following a guide carrying an umbrella, and yet here I was, proposing that we join a tour group. And not just any tour group, but one that involved a coach, and, quite possibly, someone with a microphone at the front.

"An organised tour?" Michael said. "As in one that could have pensioners and children in tow?"

I nodded. It sounded hellish.

"And what's the other option?"

I shrugged. "We take a bus to a place called Pazin, which is about halfway to the Slovenian border. And then we somehow catch a train to a town near Bled, where we can hopefully flag down a taxi. The problem with this, though, is the train takes five-and-a-half hours."

Michael inhaled sharply. "Let's take an organised tour."

6

At number 5 Decumanus Street was the striking Gothic House. Two rows of arched windows adorned with flowerpots dominated the building. Built in 1473, in a Venetian style, it once was the home of a wealthy family from medieval Porec. Nowadays, a shop filled its lower floor, selling T-shirts and postcards. Most of the T-shirts had images of cannabis leaves or Che Guevara on them.

"So what are we looking for now?" I asked Michael. The midday sun was baking my neck, and I was getting sick of the crowds filling every street. Michael was rushing past them, a man on a mission.

"The basilica," he said, barely audible over the din of clattering shoes, crying children and street hawkers. "It's around this corner."

A basilica is an important church that a Pope has given special ceremonial rights to. Porec's Euphrasian Basilica was built between 543 and 554 by Bishop Euphrasius. It contained a cathedral, an atrium, a baptistery, a bell tower, and an Episcopal palace, whatever one of those was. UNESCO had deemed the Euphrasian Basilica such a significant early Christian site that it had placed it on their World Heritage List.

I had to admit that the entrance to the basilica looked good, but, like everywhere else in Porec, it was crowded. A golden mosaic depicting Jesus hung above an arched stone gateway, his face sombre as he stared at the cheap restaurant next door. The message above him read: *I am the gate. Who enters through me will be saved.*

We jostled with the crowd to squeeze through, finding ourselves in an atrium festooned with columns and religious icons. A bell tower adjoined the atrium, but Michael and I entered the church to our right.

The interior was mainly mosaics and arches, with tourists clamouring for the best possible photo positions. In their midst sat people praying, reminding us that the basilica was actually a working church. "Let's go," I said. "Let's leave these people in peace."

Outside, Michael told me that the Euphrasian Basilica was one of the best examples of early Byzantine architecture.

I sniggered at Michael's comment. He sounded like he was some kind of expert. "And what does that mean exactly?" I asked him.

"It means it's from the Later Roman Empire, when their capital was Constantinople."

I rubbed my forehead, checking for sunburn. "How do you know that?"

"From reading."

"Okay, so give me another example of early Byzantine architecture."

"The Hagia Sophia in Istanbul."

"Fair enough; I bow down."

We walked off to find some lunch.

7

"I'm sick of greasy food," I said, pushing my fork into a large slice of aubergine, watching as the oil pooled to the surface. The chips were just as bad, and the only thing I could eat was the chicken. Michael had no such difficulties. Only an oil-coated plate remained in front of him, and a set of fish bones.

With my stomach swirling, we wandered to Liberty Square, an area dominated by a large pink-and-yellow church. Around the edge of the square were more cafes and tourist shops. Predictably, the place was heaving with people, most sitting in the cafes or on some steps. After perusing some fridge magnets and postcards, we decided to find Porec's oldest square.

Unlike Liberty Square, Marafor Square was more refined and less touristy. A few outdoor bars lay at the far reaches of the square, but there were no people eating ice creams. After Michael had finished taking a hundred photos of some Roman stonework, we walked down a narrow path towards some actual Roman ruins.

The ruins were from an ancient Roman place of worship. Neptune's Temple had originally been erected in the first-century AD, but all that remained were a few broken columns and walls. It was scattered across an overgrown field.

Nearby were the remains of the Temple of Mars, which had once been the largest Roman shrine on the eastern Adriatic coast, no less. In England, the remains would form the centrepiece of an expensive museum, but here in Porec, it was just another section of the old town. Houses backed onto the temple, with washing flapping in the warm breeze. A dog ambled through, sniffing leaves and old stone.

After I'd circled the bits and pieces, I sat down and waited for Michael to finish. I checked my phone and realised free Wi-Fi was coming from somewhere.

"Michael," I shouted ten minutes later. He was framing a shot of some Roman rubble.

"Hang on," he said, angling his camera. He finished then bounded over. "What?"

"How do you fancy flying to Dubrovnik instead of getting a bus? I've just checked online, and we can get a Croatia Airlines flight for sixty quid each. We'd have to swap planes in Zagreb, but all in all, it'll be less than three hours. Much better than ten hours by bus."

"Sixty quid?"

"Yeah."

Michael put his camera in his bag and looked at me. "What time's the flight?"

I clicked my phone to check the website again. "4.30pm. Arrive in Dubrovnik at about 7pm."

Michael smiled. "Let's get it booked!"

8

Later that evening, we headed into Porec town to sample some Croatian nightlife. We found an outdoor cafe off Liberty Square and ordered a couple of Ozujskos. They came with a complimentary bowl of crisps.

Across from us, a couple of men dressed as medieval knights were having a mock battle, their swords clashing with staged grunts. A crowd had gathered around them, families enjoying the last of the sun before nightfall.

"Do you know what I like about this place?" said Michael. "There are no drunken louts anywhere. There's no one wandering around with a bottle of beer in their hand. There are no McDonald's, and no one is shouting or screaming. It's a bit classier than that."

A group of young men and women wandered past, all of them dressed up and chatting quietly. More than likely, they would end up in Byblos later that night, the biggest nightclub in town. But there was no way Michael and I were going there. As well as being fifteen years too old, we had to be up early the next morning. Country number four of the Odyssey was on the horizon - Slovenia.

4. Bled, Slovenia

Interesting fact: Slovenia has a festival dedicated to cabbages.

The coach picked us up at 8am, and, as we'd predicted, it was filled with holidaymakers, some armed with flasks and day bags. At the third hotel of the pickup routine, no one got on. Instead, the coach waited. And then waited some more.

"We are waiting for two more passengers," explained the young Croatian woman acting as our guide. Her name was Ivanah, and like many other young Croatian women, she was dark-haired and slender. She had a microphone.

Five minutes later, everyone watched as Ivanah climbed off the coach and entered the foyer of the hotel. With audible tut-tutting and groans, we waited for her to reappear, which she did, with a middle-aged couple in tow. Both looked stressed to the gills. We all stared as the woman said something to her husband. Judging from his expression, it wasn't anything nice.

As the two latecomers made their way onto the coach, all eyes were upon them. I was glaring in what I hoped conveyed annoyance. The woman looked suitably embarrassed, and kept her gaze directed at the floor. The man was braver and looked up. "So this is what it feels like," he said, "to do the Walk of Shame."

Finally, the coach moved off, destination: Slovenia.

2

Slovenia, lying between the Alps and the Mediterranean, is a small country dominated by mountains and rivers. Forest covers half its area.

During its history, Slovenia has been part of the Roman Empire, the Austria-Hungary Empire, and of course, the Socialist Federal Republic of Yugoslavia, where it was the most productive member. Its industrial output eclipsed Serbia fourfold and, compared to struggling Macedonia, Slovenia was twenty times better off.

After World War II (where Slovenia had been under German and Italian control), the country got on with rebuilding its industry. With a highly educated and skilled population, it didn't take long for Slovenia to get back on track. Productivity increased massively, so much so that, by the time of Tito's death in 1980, dissension began brewing. Many Slovenians thought it unfair that they were propping up the economies of the weaker Yugoslav states.

By 1987, Slovenia was holding mass demonstrations, demanding independence. In the spring of 1989, changes were made to the constitution, and, by June 1991, Slovenia decided enough was enough, and declared itself an independent country.

Two days later, the Yugoslav People's Army mobilised itself to teach the upstarts a lesson. In Belgrade, politicians believed that the mere presence of Yugoslav troops on Slovenian soil would make the people of Slovenia quiver with fear. They were wrong in this assumption.

3

Initially, Yugoslav helicopters began dropping leaflets across Slovenia, saying: *We invite you to peace and cooperation,* which sounded quite nice and heartfelt. The second part of the message was a bit harsher: *All resistance will be crushed.*

In response, the Slovenian government told Belgrade to cease the helicopter sorties. When the flights continued, the Slovenians shot two of them down. It was an unprecedented move, and one that shocked Belgrade. And, while the Yugoslav generals scratched their heads, the small Slovenian army began attacking Yugoslav troops along the border. That was it, Belgrade decided. The soft approach hadn't worked, and so they ordered the Yugoslav army in. It was time to crush the resistance.

Troops and tanks advanced into Slovenia, quickly overrunning the small pockets of Slovenian opposition they found. The People's Army forged towards the main airport. They took it easily.

The next day, the tide turned. The Slovenians somehow pushed the might of the Yugoslav army into retreat. The Slovenian troops were all highly motivated and keen to fight for their country's freedom, whereas the Yugoslav troops were mostly conscripts, away from home, with little incentive to fight against men who only months beforehand had been their allies. Both sides began battling in earnest.

With a full-blown war on their doorstep, the EU had no choice but to step in. They ordered an immediate ceasefire, but both sides ignored the order; then, in a key battle, the Slovenian army won back the airport.

The next day, the Slovenians captured over 400 Yugoslav men, plus nine tanks. The tiny man of Yugoslavia was showing some sharp teeth indeed. And so it continued for another few days, with Yugoslav troops suffering setbacks and losses. By 4th July, Belgrade agreed to a ceasefire and, a few days later, the Ten-Day War ended with a resounding Slovenian victory. But Belgrade had bigger fish to fry – most notably Croatia, where a terrible and longer war was about to take place.

As for Slovenia, the world recognised its independence, and the nation got back to what it did best – increasing its industrial output. In 2004, it joined NATO, and, four years later, became the first former communist nation to join the euro zone. According to the Global Peace Index of 2012, Slovenia is now one of the most peaceful countries in the world.

4

Getting into Slovenia involved the first overland border crossing of the Odyssey. The coach stopped at the Dragonia border point, and a uniformed woman got on and wandered down the aisles to have a look at everyone's passport. No one was thrown off, not even the two latecomers, and we were soon on our way into a new country, passing the flag of Slovenia flapping above the blue of the EU flag.

The view outside quickly began to change. Mediterranean scrub made way for conifers and hills. Before long, we were travelling through alpine scenery straight from the *Sound of Music*.

"So, welcome to Slovenia," said Ivanah. "And let me tell you some things about this beautiful country."

We all listened as Ivanah told us about the population (about 2 million), some basic geography (mountains and forest) and about the wildlife of Slovenia. "It has deer, boar and lynx," she said, "and small numbers of wolves and bears. But perhaps Slovenia's most famous creature is the *olm*, a blind amphibian that lives in a cave."

While we all thought about blind amphibians and packs of wolves, the coach lumbered onwards along a well-maintained Slovenian road. Michael was already reading his latest science-fiction novel, and so I put my iPod on, settling back in my seat.

5

Two hours later, we arrived in the capital of Slovenia, Ljubljana. It was right in the middle of the country, which meant we were getting close to Bled. Ivanah's microphone crackled back into life.

"We have no time to stop in Ljubljana, but our driver will go through some parts for you. This way, you will see how pretty the city is. And perhaps another time you can visit for longer."

I was quite sad to see the Slovenian capital passing by so quickly. But, from what I could gather, it was a pretty town, distinctly European, with church spires, bridges and grand old buildings everywhere to see. It even had a castle perched on a hill. All too quickly, though, we were driving out through the outskirts, and then, an hour later, we arrived at our destination - the alpine town of Bled. All thoughts of Ljubljana vanished. Bled was stunning.

6

Bled is located in the Julian Alps, just thirty kilometres south of the Austrian border. It is one of Slovenia's prime tourist destinations, mainly because of its large glacial lake. The natural beauty of the town and its surrounds has meant that rich and famous people have often stayed in Bled.

In the 19th century, it was the Austrian Empire's finest health resort, and, when Josip Tito was in charge, he made Lake Bled his personal place of retreat. He often met heads of states there. Prince Charles and Donald Trump had once stayed in a Bled hotel, though not at the same time.

"First I take you to castle," announced Ivanah. She gestured out of the window towards a spectacular sight. There was a rich babble of conversation from inside the coach as everybody stared up at the wonder.

The castle was perched high upon a rocky outcrop, flanked with lush conifers. If a dragon had suddenly appeared with a hobbit strapped to its back, it would not have looked out of place.

"We will drive most of the way, but then we will have to walk. But only for about a hundred metres. It will not be too difficult, I hope. And the view from the top will take your breath away."

Ten minutes later, the walk was taking my breath away. But others were finding it much harder. The woman in front of Michael and me was wheezing and panting like a rabid horse. When she stopped to catch her breath, she looked on the edge of a heart attack. Her husband didn't look much better, but in the end, everyone made it to the top without incident.

The castle was exactly how a castle ought to be: full of cone-shaped turrets, high stone walls and a moat with a drawbridge. We entered its courtyard and followed Ivanah to the edge, a section that overlooked the lake. The view was one of the most amazing I'd seen. The water was a beautiful turquoise, flanked by dense green hills, and further back were the jagged cliffs of the Julian

Mountains. We could also see Slovenia's solitary island, a tiny outcrop at the far end of the lake with a church in the middle. Bled was a picture postcard from every angle we cared to look.

"We got married here fourteen years ago," said a man to my left. His wife was by his side, with a small boy stood between them. "It's just as beautiful as it was then."

His wife smiled. "And do you know which word is in the middle of Slovenia?" she asked cryptically.

I looked at Michael. He seemed as befuddled as me.

"Love!" she said. "S-LOVE-enia!"

I looked for a bucket to vomit into.

7

Half an hour later, we were back in the town of Bled, wandering around by ourselves. Ivanah had given us one hour before we had to regroup. There wasn't much to see, apart from a large Slovenian bank building, and some fish at the edge of the lake, so Michael and I found a cafe to get some lunch.

"Your snoring was bad last night," Michael said. "It woke me up a few times. I think I need to buy some earplugs."

I knew I snored. My wife berated me about it considerably. In fact, it surprised me that Michael hadn't said anything before.

"Good idea," I said, trying to extract some fish from the pile of bones on my plate. "But I'd just like to say at this point that your toes woke *me* up last night."

Michael sniggered. "Sorry?"

"In the middle of the night, your toes touched mine, and they woke me up. It was...distressing."

Michael sniggered some more, and so did I.

When we had first arrived at our cheap hotel in Porec, both of us were alarmed to find that our room had only one bed in it, albeit a double bed. After explaining things to the woman behind the desk in the foyer, she'd clicked her computer and found us another room. But this one contained only a single bed. "We will get one more bed for you," she said. "No problem."

But there was a problem. The new room was so narrow that we had to squash the second bed at the end of the first bed. When the woman left, Michael and I regarded our sleeping arrangements. As it stood, we could either sleep with our heads almost touching, our feet almost touching, or a mixture of feet and heads in close proximity.

"I'm not having my head next to your stinking feet," I said, already picking up my pillow and moving it to the opposite end of the bed. "And I don't want my head near your head. You might have lice."

Michael picked up his pillow, and moved it to the opposite end of his bed too. That done, we went out for a few beers, neither of us knowing that a game of slumber-fuelled footsie would ensue later that night.

8

After lunch, we went to find a pharmacy. It was faintly amusing watching Michael mime that he wanted some earplugs to the dazzled shop assistant, but in the end, he got them. We then rejoined our group for a trip to the island in the middle of Lake Bled.

Getting to it meant a ride in a gondola-type boat called a pletna. As the sixteen of us sat down in the vessel, a boatman took up station at the back and began rowing us softly towards our destination. Over on our right was the castle, still looking as impressive as it had done before lunch.

The journey was tranquil (except for a couple of kids hankering for a drink from mum and dad). It was just the quiet slosh of the oars and a few calls from the swans by the shoreline. As we approached the island, Ivanah spoke up.

"The island has ninety-nine steps. They lead up to the church. And it is a custom here in Bled that, during a wedding, the husband must carry his bride up the steps, while she remains silent. This will guarantee a long-lasting marriage." We regarded the steps.

"And there is a legend," Ivanah said a few seconds later. "Hundreds of years ago, a rich woman died and gave all her jewellery to the church. The priests decided to melt it down to make a church bell. When it was finished, everyone was happy. It was going to look great in the church spire."

Michael suddenly stood up to take a photo of the spire, causing a moment of panic from the woman sitting next to him, due to the slight wobble he caused. I'd wisely elected to sit opposite Michael, knowing he'd be itching to take some snaps on the short journey across. Satisfied with his photo, he sat back down, allowing Ivanah to continue with the tale.

"The priests brought builders to the island. As they moved the bell into position, something terrible happened. The bell dropped, and then rolled to the lake. It sank to the bottom."

We all looked over the edge to stare down into the green water, but of course there was no sign of the bell, because, as Ivanah had already pointed out, the story was a legend.

"And now," she said ominously. "Locals say that if the wind is just right, then the bell can be heard below the surface, playing a sad song for the dead woman."

"Boo!" I shouted.

Except I didn't.

9

After reaching the island, we began to climb the steps. They were not as bad as first feared, although I was thankful not to be carrying anyone up them. Michael was already way in front, camera in hand, snapping anything that seemed worthy of his attention.

When I reached the 99th step, I was out of breath and in need of a drink. I took a long sip of my water, and found Michael standing beside the tall spire of the Assumption of Mary's Pilgrimage Church. It was pinkish in colour, with a nice little clock underneath some arched windows. It also had a bell, I noticed.

"You took your time," he said.

We went inside, following some other tour group members. It was small but beautiful, full of golden icons. It was also packed with people deep in prayer. They didn't seem to mind that a bunch of tourists had just invaded their peaceful sanctuary; they were probably used to it. We left the church and had a quick wander around the tiny island, but there wasn't that much more to see. We headed back down the steps to wait for the return journey.

10

An hour later, Ivanah was leading us through a shopping arcade in downtown Bled. "It is time for the cream cakes," she told us. "Bled is famous for its vanilla-and-cream cakes. You will all get one as part of the tour."

The owners of the cafe had a well-prepared racket going on. Before we'd arrived, no one was sitting in their cafe, but, after two tour groups arrived simultaneously, the place was packed. The staff were clearly veterans of mass arrival, because they sprang to action immediately, setting out serviettes and plates, rushing here and there, preparing everything with speed and well-practised ease.

Five minutes later, the cakes arrived. They looked like chunkier versions of a custard slice, something I tried to avoid in England. As I have never been a fan of custard, the Slovenian Supercake did not appeal to me.

"Mnmmm," said Michael, licking his chops after taking a large bite of his cake. "Nice!"

I prodded the side of my cake, pressing my finger into the yellow section. The cream layer above looked okay, as did the icing sugar on top, but it was the custard I was worried about.

"Don't worry," said Ivanah, noting the look on my face. "These are not like your cakes back home. They are...how do you say...lighter. Try it and see. They taste amazing!"

I did so, finding out it was actually quite good, and nothing like a custard slice. Michael had already finished his and was now taking some photos of mine.

"Get lost," I said. "Let me eat my cake in peace." Michael ignored me and took another photo.

Twenty minutes later, we were all done and ready to leave. Our day trip to Slovenia had been a fun one. We boarded the coach for the return trip to Porec. One night there, and then we would head for the airport. Dubrovnik was our next port of call.

5. Dubrovnik, Croatia

Interesting fact: Dalmatian dogs originated from Dalmatia, in southern Croatia.

"Ladies and gentlemen," said the raspy voice from the flight deck, "this is your captain speaking. Due to high winds at Dubrovnik Airport, we have no choice but to divert to Split. Coaches will be available to take you onwards to Dubrovnik. Sorry for the inconvenience."

I rolled my eyes at Michael. "Bloody hell," I said. "So much for saving time by flying. Now we'll have a four-hour coach journey - at least."

Michael said nothing, and turned to stare out of the window.

"Aren't you bothered?" I asked.

"Yeah. But what can we do?"

I closed my book and looked at my watch. With a bit of luck, we'd be in Dubrovnik by midnight.

2

Dubrovnik is Croatia's jewel in the crown, a UNESCO heritage site that once rivalled Venice as an Adriatic city-state.

As well as its well-preserved old town, it has beaches and long stretches of coastline. When Irish playwright George Bernard Shaw visited the city in 1929, he said, *'If you want to see heaven on earth, come to Dubrovnik.'* If Shaw had visited 63 years later, he might have described it differently.

War broke out in 1991, after Croatia declared itself independent from Yugoslavia. Serbs living in Croatia at the time (making up 12% of the population) didn't take too kindly to this announcement, and demanded that Belgrade do something.

After finishing the Ten-Day War with Slovenia, the Yugoslav army headed south. They had hundreds of tanks and jet aircraft at their disposal (even though most of them were almost thirty years old), and were confident of victory, especially since they knew the Croatians only had a few old tanks and some biplanes that had been used for crop dusting. It seemed the war would be David versus Goliath, especially when the Montenegrins joined on the Serb side. And so it started out to be.

By October, Serb and Montenegrin troops had reached Dubrovnik. With only a handful of Croat soldiers inside the city, the Serbs were bargaining on an easy victory. Air strikes knocked out the water and electricity supply, and troops secured the highways. It was only day three of the battle, and Dubrovnik was already under siege.

The people of Dubrovnik refused to submit, so the Serbs and Montenegrins began shelling the city and setting up sniper nests in the hills. As Serbian troops tightened the net, they displaced thousands of Croatian citizens, who immediately became war refugees. Meanwhile, in Dubrovnik itself, Croatians were in dire need of supplies. In a moment of mercy, Serb and Montenegrin forces allowed humanitarian aid to arrive by ship. These ships then took thousands of refugees away with them.

By December, with no sign of surrender, mortar fire and snipers began targeting the old town. Some civilians were killed in the attacks, but Croatian forces rallied and managed to push the Serbs back. By May 1992, Serb and Montenegrin forces retreated, and the Siege of Dubrovnik officially ended.

As the dust cleared, the people of the city discovered that over half the buildings in the old town had suffered some sort of damage, with one in ten suffering heavy damage. Worse, some important palaces had burned to the ground, and many museums, businesses and homes had been looted. There was only one thing left to do – start rebuilding.

3

Split airport spat us out into a terminal full of confused passengers. As well as our flight, other planes had diverted, and now everyone was baffled about what to do. No one from the airline was there to greet us, and no one seemed to be organising onwards travel. I decided to step outside and speak to a white-haired man smoking a cigarette. He was standing next to a coach.

"Are you going to Dubrovnik?"

The man regarded me and took another deep drag. "Eh?"

"Is this bus going to Dubrovnik?"

The man nodded.

Okay, I thought. The coach *was* going to Dubrovnik, but was it the correct one? As far as I could tell, no one was aboard yet, so maybe it was a normal scheduled service that wouldn't be leaving for ages. I decided to clarify. After all, I didn't want to pay for a journey that the airline had said would be free. "Is this for the Zagreb flight that was diverted?"

"Zagreb, yes."

"And it's going to Dubrovnik?"

"Dubrovnik, yes! Zagreb, yes!"

"Is it free?"

"Of course!"

The man was clearly a nutcase, so I sought out Michael, and told him of my conversation.

"So we're either going to Zagreb or Dubrovnik," he said. "Or possibly both, but at least we can sit down and dump our bags."

We walked out, shoved our bags in the compartment, and climbed aboard. The man had already lit another cigarette and said nothing as we did so, merely watching. But after seeing our bold action, other passengers began to do the same thing, and soon the coach was full. With a last drag of his cigarette, the man stamped it under his foot, and climbed aboard. The engine was started, and off we set.

The majority of other passengers seemed locals, and after only a few minutes, the length of the coach was engulfed in deep foreign conversation. That was something we had noticed about people in the Balkans: they certainly enjoyed a good natter. We sat back and wondered where we were going.

4

Limestone mountains on one side, and sea on the other, flanked the road we were travelling along. The main industry, at least near Split Airport, seemed to be cement factories, but, as we got closer to the city, things looked a little better. Large *Tommy* hypermarkets came into view, as did a huge stadium across the bay. We rumbled past Split and then turned towards Zagreb.

Michael had noticed the sign for Zagreb too. Zagreb, the Croatian capital, was at the opposite end of the country to Dubrovnik, up near the Slovenian border. It was where we had changed planes. If we were returning to Zagreb first, which it appeared we were, then it would be a four-hour journey, followed by a further seven hours to Dubrovnik. It didn't bear thinking about.

But what could we do? Hijack the bus and demand to be let out in the hope of flagging down a taxi? No, we had no choice but to sit back and accept things. Just then, an elderly man, sitting two seats in front of us, shuffled forward to the driver. After engaging him in conversation for a few moments, he made his way back down the aisle and took his seat.

Ten minutes later, we passed through a little village nestled between some mountainous terrain. The coach pulled over to the side of the road. Everyone had a look at the nice little river and simple homesteads. There was even a little church perched up on some rocks. It was a beautiful Croatian village. We all wondered what was going on.

The old man got up and walked to the front of the coach. With a hiss of hydraulic air, the doors whooshed open, and he stepped outside. As the coach lumbered back into the road, he waved us off. It seemed the diverted flight had been a Godsend for the man. We had dropped him off in his own village.

5

The decrepit Yugo swerved around the coach like it was being driven by the devil himself. It was flashing its headlights, and going hell for leather as it passed us.

"Maniac," I said, as I was pushed back into my seat due to the centrifugal force of the coach's passage up the mountain. "Overtaking on a blind bend like that. He should be locked up."

Suddenly, with an almighty hiss of brakes, we decelerated. At first I thought we were about to hit something, but when I looked through the big window at the front, I could see the Yugo driver. He'd stopped some distance ahead and was frantically waving his arms. Perhaps we were going to be hijacked after all.

When we came to a standstill, a passenger in the Yugo got out of the car and joined the driver. It was the same old man we had deposited in the village behind us. With a big embarrassed smile, he climbed on board, spoke to the driver, then shuffled down the aisle, saying things in Croatian to those nearby. People laughed. Then he reached up into the overhead compartment and retrieved his coat.

The journey continued.

6

Whilst Michael flicked through some of his photos, I stared outside. We were tearing around mountain curves with sheer drops on one side, and steep rocky cliff faces on the other. Signs warned of potential rock falls, which I thought was a waste of time: a warning about a train crossing coming up, yes; possible livestock in the road ahead, yes; rocks about to fall on your head and kill you, no! It wasn't like there was anything I (or the driver, for that matter) could do about it. So what was the point?

After a sweeping manoeuvre around another curving road, we came to a junction of sorts. One sign said Zagreb, the other Dubrovnik. I waited with trepidation for the driver to make his choice. I was delighted when he chose Dubrovnik. There was some light at the end of the tunnel.

A long while later, we came to what I presumed was another tollbooth. We'd already passed a few of them since joining the road to Dubrovnik. But it wasn't a tollbooth: it was a Croatian border point. The coach stopped, and the driver spoke to someone in the little hatch. Then we set off again. I wondered where we were. And then we came to the next border, the country on the other side.

"We're going into Bosnia," I told Michael, jolting him from his book.

"What?"

"We're entering Bosnia! Look!"

The border point was like the Croatian one, except for the blue and yellow Bosnian flag. No passports were collected or checked, just a brief stop at the hatch, and we trundled through.

"I know where we are," said Michael, pointing at the sea on our right-hand side. "Bosnia has a tiny bit of coastline, only about 10 or 12 miles, I think. That's where we are."

Bosnia was getting dark. And it didn't take long to get back into Croatia. And then, four hours after leaving Split Airport, we arrived in Dubrovnik.

7

"So how was my snoring last night?" I asked Michael over breakfast.

"Fine. I had my ear plugs in."

I recalled a time in Amsterdam when I hadn't been so lucky with snoring. I'd been nineteen at the time, away with some university friends for a few days of fun in the Dutch capital.

Being tight on budget, we'd ignored the hotels and opted for an establishment called Bob's Youth Hostel. The four of us were each given a bed in a large dormitory dominated by young American backpacker types. They were always up at the crack of dawn with whoops and yays, hogging the shared bathroom with glee.

Because we hadn't booked the beds in advance, all four of us were split up around the large dorm, but I'd managed to bag a top bunk. One night, when I climbed up, the young man on my left was asleep and snoring. The bloke on my right was fast asleep too, his dreadlocks crumpled around his pillow. I switched off my light and drifted towards slumber.

Sometime later, my head was battered from a sideways blow.

"What the...?" I shrieked, sitting upright and switching on my travel light. Mr Dreadlock was sitting up too, pillow in hand – his weapon of choice. He was staring at me with a confused expression. The snoring man was still snoring, oblivious to the events unfolding only metres away from his grunts and sniffles.

"Sorry, mate," Mr Dreadlock said, in an Aussie accent. "I thought the snoring was coming from you." He flopped back down and so did I. Sleep took a long time to come, with snoring from one side, and the threat of a pillow attack from the other.

8

On the way to the old town, Michael and I passed teams of men toiling over road equipment; they were causing hellish snarls of traffic. We didn't mind though, and sidestepped the cones with ease.

Further along, I saw a man carrying a large bucket filled with tools. He was aged about forty, and had tightly shaven hair. As he walked in front of us, I couldn't help notice the deep scars on his scalp. Two almost parallel furrows ran vertically down the back of his head, making me wonder how he'd received them. In the siege of Dubrovnik, the man would have been in his early twenties, prime fighting age. Or perhaps he'd suffered shrapnel wounds from a mortar attack. Whatever the reason, he looked fit and healthy, and Michael and I soon passed him. We headed towards the entrance of the old town.

The sun was out, and I could tell Michael was eager to get in. He'd read about some museums inside the tightly packed cobblestone streets of the old town, and I knew we would have to visit at least one of them.

Dubrovnik's old town was gorgeous. At the other side of a gate, we found ourselves at the start of Stradun, the main street. Limestone pavement stretched in a straight line towards a tall bell tower at the other end. Citrus trees cloaked some nearby buildings in green, fruit hanging merrily from their branches. It was hard to believe that Serb and Montenegrin forces had directed mortar fire onto this very street.

While Michael took some photos of a structure called Onofrio's Fountain, I studied the map, quickly noting that one of Europe's oldest surviving pharmacies was in the vicinity. I spotted a sign for it down a short, narrow alleyway. I called Michael over and we both headed in. "There's a museum down here, too," Michael added, noticing a sign.

The pharmacy turned out to be disappointing. Instead of leeches and strange potions, it contained a woman in a lab coat selling another woman some headache tablets. It was just like any other pharmacy, and nothing in it seemed to suggest it was the third oldest one in Europe.

The museum was near the pharmacy, at the opposite end of an open cloister that we later found out was part of a monastery. We bought a ticket each from a man sitting at a table and entered the cloister area. It was actually rather nice, with a set of stone arches and columns surrounding an area of greenery.

At the entrance to the museum, another man waited. Michael was about to show him our tickets, but the man waved them away. "I don't need to see tickets," he said. "We are not Germany."

It seemed a strange thing to say, but we thanked the man anyway, and stepped inside. It was full of old pots, which Michael reckoned had been used to store medicines from the pharmacy. It also had a collection of religious icons, which I looked at briefly before stopping at a small glass panel covering up a section of the wall. Behind it was some damage caused by a mortar attack. I stared at the hole; it was the most interesting thing in the museum.

9

We strolled along Stradun, passing tourists eating ice creams, or enjoying espressos in the sidewalk cafes. During July and August, the streets would be packed with people, most of them day-trippers from cruise ships, but with it being only April, the crowds were manageable.

Of course, there were a few tour groups in operation, most of them camera-toting Chinese tourists. A sizeable group had gathered around Orlando's Column, a four-sided stone pillar that featured a carving of a knight called Orlando. According to legend, he'd defended the city against the Saracens in the eighth century. Other tourists had gathered around an old gent playing a mournful tune on an accordion.

Michael and I sidestepped them all and entered a small exhibition located inside the 16th century Sponza Palace. The exhibition displayed photos from the Siege of Dubrovnik. All the photographs had been taken by a man called Pavo Urban, a native of Dubrovnik.

At the outbreak of the siege, Urban had been a 22-year-old student living in Zagreb. He quickly left his studies and returned to the city of his birth to work as a war photographer for a local newspaper.

One of his photographs showed thick black smoke billowing up from the port area of the old town. The caption simply read:

Dubrovnik 1991. Another of Urban's photos showed smoke rising over Stradun, the street eerily devoid of people.

One bleak photo showed three men huddled together inside a stone alcove. One was standing upright, his back pressed against a wall, his eyes downcast. The second man was crouching down, hands covering his ears. A third man was sitting on some steps, cradling a quivering dog in his arms. The blurring of one hand suggested that he had been stroking the animal when the photo was taken.

I stared at a photo of a woman carrying a baby across a rubble-infested street, and then at a strange snap of a woman sitting in an armchair. She was in a living room, but everything around her was in ruin: pictures, ornaments, walls, and even her doors - all blasted to bits.

The most moving photos were the final few. In them, Pavo was in the old town on the main street. The series showed Stradun empty, then filled with smoke after a shell had landed. It was the morning of 6th December 1991, the day of the fiercest attack on the city. The final four photos were taken nearby, close to Orlando's Column. Judging from the angle of the photos, Pavo Urban had been taking cover beside a wall.

One showed smoke from a mortar attack on the Church. The next two were almost identical, only a slight shift in location. But the final one, the last photo Pavo ever took, showed that he had left his position to get a better angle. Moments later, a shell fragment hit him in the stomach. He died, aged just 23.

10

"This is where he must've been hit," I said, finding the approximate place the young photographer had been standing.

Michael looked around and nodded assent. The wall Urban had been taking cover behind was actually a stone column that formed the entrance to a restaurant. It seemed eerie to be standing where someone had died so violently, especially with crowds of people wandering about, oblivious to it all. If Pavo had still been alive, he'd be his forties now, not much older than Michael and me. After a moment of quiet contemplation, we moved off to find a cafe.

We found one in Gundulic Square, another beautiful part of the old town, this time adjacent to a small fruit and vegetable market. A statue in the middle was of a long-haired man called Ivan Gundulic, a famous Croatian poet. We ordered a coffee each and discussed our plans for the next few days.

My idea was to hire a car the following day so we could drive to Mostar, in Bosnia. After enjoying Sarajevo so much, I was eager to see more of Bosnia & Herzegovina. We could stay there for a night and drive back to Dubrovnik the next morning. Michael agreed with this, as long as I did the driving. "The last time I drove in a foreign country, I crashed," he told me.

"Really?"

"Yeah. In Spain. Literally five minutes after driving it away from the hire car place, I crashed into a parked car. No injuries, thank God."

After getting back from Mostar, our main issue would be finding a route to Albania. It was proving to be a major headache because, as far as we could tell, no direct bus routes existed to the Albanian capital. And the only flights we had managed to find were via Vienna, with an astronomical price tag attached.

Michael got the large map out again, being careful this time not to topple my drink. While he unfolded it, I watched a couple of dogs chasing each other around a nearby table. Round and round they went, enjoying the game, until one stopped to take a detour. It squatted underneath a table, much to the horror of a nearby waitress.

"It's shitting!" she yelled to no one in particular. She ran over to the dog and waved her arms. "It's shitting!" But it was too late. The dog had done its foul deed, and was already scampering away.

"If you look here," said Michael, pointing at a road leading south from Dubrovnik, "this crosses the border into Montenegro. Then it passes through all these towns." His finger traced a route along a large bay, passing towns such as Herceg Novi and Kotor.

"We know there are buses to these places; we've seen them advertised," he said. "And from there, we'll be able to catch another bus to Albania."

"But what if we can't?"

"Look, people must go to Albania all the time, and vice versa. There's bound to be a bus. Besides, it will give us a chance to see Montenegro. We can stop in some of these towns; maybe stay over in one. Didn't you mention you wanted to go to Kotor?"

Suddenly, a squadron of pigeons descended upon the square like a scene from a Hitchcock film. Hundreds of them flew from lofty rafters, flapping their grey wings with an audible and quite scary hum. The reason for their rapid arrival was the presence of a man emptying the contents of a yellow bucket. He was causing a pigeon feeding frenzy.

I looked back at Michael. "Yeah, Kotor would be great. But it's the bus to Albania I'm worried about."

When the bill arrived, Michael and I were in for a shock. Two coffees had cost almost seven pounds. Long gone were the times when Croatia was a cheap destination.

11

After a walk around the entire length of the old city walls - where we'd seen washing hanging from lines, numerous lounging cats, and an American family trying to use one of those telescope things, but failing dismally – we stood and pondered what to do next. We both decided it was food time and so ambled around the old town to scope out suitable places.

The first place we tried looked nice and upmarket. Its speciality was fish, and, after the waiter had given us the menus, I was eager to see what was on offer.

"*Jesus!*" I whispered to Michael. "Have you seen the prices?" Most of the main courses were about 350 kuna, about thirty-five pounds, well above our budget for a quick lunch.

"I can't even afford a starter," whispered Michael, swivelling his head to see where the waiter was.

After a quick glance myself, I leaned towards Michael. "Let's run for it."

We got up and moved rapidly, but unstealthily, away from the table until we rounded an alleyway to make our escape. That done, we slowed and came to a hatch selling pizza slices for only a few pounds each. They were delicious. We went off to find a hire car company for our journey to Mostar the next day.

12

In a bar that night, we planned our route. After crossing into Bosnia, we would head northeast until we came to a town called Trebinje. After that, it would be easy, just stick on the same highway all the way to Mostar. A journey of around two hours, we reckoned.

"Hello?" said a man on the next table. He looked about fifty, and was sitting alone smoking a cigarette. His accent suggested he was Croatian.

We both looked over, wondering what he wanted.

"Are you driving to Mostar?"

I nodded uncertainly. The last thing we needed was a hitchhiker.

"In hire car with Croatian plates?"

I nodded again.

"I am taxi driver," the man said. "I have driven to Mostar many times. And the route you have chosen is not quickest, but I agree that it is maybe the best. The road is good all the way. But I think the only problem you will have is with police."

"The police?" I said.

The man nodded. "The police in Bosnia like to stop people. They give big fine for nothing. I was driving to Sarajevo – not as taxi driver – but with my wife to see her sister. Two policemen stop me, and say I did not have correct papers to drive through Bosnia. I told them I did. The police say I must pay 50 euro!"

Michael and I whistled. I'd actually read that the Bosnian police could be a little overzealous with foreign-registered cars. One American couple I'd read about had been forced to pay a fine for not having yellow high-visibility jackets in the car with them. Another tourist had been fined for not having his lights on, even though it had been lunchtime.

"I tell them no way! I have papers, *look!* But they say I must pay 50 euro, or else drive with them to speak with boss. They say boss might give bigger fine! What could I do, eh? My wife was saying, pay them, but I felt angry. In the end, I argue, and they reduce fine to 30 euro, which I pay. They let me go. So what I'm saying is, watch out for Bosnian police."

We thanked the man and finished our drinks. It was time to pack for Mostar.

6. Mostar, Bosnia & Herzegovina

Interesting fact: Herzegovina, the southern part of the country, means Duke's Land.

We picked up the hire car, and after filling it with our stuff, we were off: me driving, Michael chief navigator.

The Bosnian border wasn't actually that far from Dubrovnik, just a few miles inland from the coast, but, to get to it, we had to climb the car through a series of steep turns; all flanked with mountainous countryside and cypress trees. With the Adriatic behind us, we came to the border.

The Croatian side looked modern and slick, with a petrol station-type roof that covered both sides of the road. The Bosnian side was simpler: just a hut and a couple of uniformed men. But both sides were equally efficient, and so, for the third time in the Odyssey, Michael and I entered Bosnia & Herzegovina.

The road, even though it was supposedly a main highway, was a twisting and turning single-lane sliver of tarmac. Whenever we came up behind a slow-moving truck (which we did frequently), a nerve-shattering overtaking manoeuvre would ensue. Inches separated us as I steered our car past, trying to avoid contact with the truck, while, at the same time, attempting to keep the wheels off the dusty roadside verge.

The Bosnian countryside was mainly limestone hills and the occasional tiny village, most of which looked as if they hadn't changed in hundreds of years. But one thing we noticed was the number of 1980s Volkswagen Golf Mark IIs. They were everywhere, all driven by men, and all going strong, despite their age. From our rough estimate, it seemed that three out of every five cars in Bosnia was a VW Golf. It was only later that we learned that a large car factory had existed in Sarajevo before the war, churning out Golfs for the Yugoslav market. Between 1985 and

1992, Bosnia had been making 25,000 of them a year. No wonder so many still survived.

Suddenly we passed a large white sign splashed with Cyrillic. Underneath it read: *Welcome to Republic of Srpska.*

"What the hell is the Republic of Srpska?" I asked Michael.

"Now that's an interesting question."

2

"When Bosnia was part of Yugoslavia," Michael told me, as he sat back in his seat, pleased as ever that he could enlighten me about something, "the three main ethnic groups - Muslims, Serbs and Croats - were all given equal rights and representation. But when independence was being talked about, the Serbs got worried. They thought the Muslim majority would hold all the cards, so they decided to form their own part of Bosnia."

I slowed down so I could overtake a woman leading a line of goats and sheep along the road. The goats had big floppy ears, and some of the sheep had cute lambs following them.

"The Serbian sections of Bosnia were mainly in the north and west, and, when Bosnia did go independent, the Serbs living there refused to accept it. They called themselves the Republic of Srpska. Radovan Karadzic became their first president."

"And that's what kick-started the Bosnian War?"

"Exactly. Both factions of Bosnia were fighting against one another. But the Republic of Srpska had the backing of Belgrade."

"So it was in these Serbian sections of Bosnia that most of the ethnic cleansing happened?"

"Correct."

"So why," I asked, "does the Republic of Srpska still exist, even though the war finished in 1995?"

"Because, as part of the peace agreement, the Republic of Srpska had to be recognised as an individual political entity. For instance, they have their own flag, their own police and courts, and they have their own president. They even have their own capital city – somewhere in the north, I think."

I wondered how relations were between both factions.

"Okay, I think," said Michael. "Both armies merged a few years ago, so things can't be that bad. But the Republic of Srpska does still act like an autonomous state."

3

"By the way, your snoring was bad last night," announced Michael. Both of us had been silent for a while as we drove through tiny hamlets with bell-necklaced cows and parked VW Golfs. As we'd descended through the mountains, the rocky crags had given way to fields, rivers and vineyards.

"What about your ear plugs?"

"I had them in, but your snoring still penetrated them. I think you need an operation or something."

A man in the middle of the road caught my attention. I strained to see what he was doing, but he was too far away. Michael was no help: his eyesight was worse than mine. Then, before we could take action, we saw it was a police roadblock. Immediately I pressed on the brakes, wondering whether I'd been exceeding the speed limit. The policeman watched us approach, but then moved to the side of the road, gesturing that we should carry on. I did so, heading onwards to the town on Trebinje.

Trebinje was actually the sixth biggest city in the Republic of Srpska, but Michael and I didn't see much of the historical centre, because we merely skirted around one edge. But we did see a dark-haired man drive his VW Golf the wrong way around a roundabout so that he didn't have to go all the way around. Never mind that he almost crashed into us; as long as he could save himself a few seconds, that was okay.

As we made our way up a hill lined with houses and a few shops, we ended up stuck behind a Yugo going at 5mph. Its lawnmower engine screamed as it made its way up the incline, but its two passengers seemed not bothered in the slightest. A swift overtaking movement, and we were on our way, the passage to Mostar now a simple case of sticking to the same road.

At some point, we left the Republic of Srpska and entered Herzegovina. It was here that the police stopped us. An officer with a large baton in his hand gestured that we should pull over.

As the policeman moved to my window, I looked at his accomplice on the other side of the road. Both men were watching me carefully as I pressed the button to lower my window.

The first policeman stared at me, then Michael, then back at me again. He looked around the inside of the car for a moment, and then finally addressed me in a language I couldn't understand.

"We are English," I said to him, smiling. "From England."

The man scrunched his face slightly and his shoulders slumped. Without saying another word, he waved his baton, indicating that I should drive on. I thanked him, raised the window and did just that. From the rear-view mirror, I could see the other officer raise his palms in the air, as if to say, *Why did you let them go?* Whatever the reason, Michael and I continued with our journey, and arrived in Mostar just after 1pm. We found a guesthouse with a spare room, and then went out to see the sights.

4

Mostar was beautiful. It was even more stunning than Dubrovnik, full of winding cobblestone alleys with Turkish-style bazaars, and small coffee houses where people sat drinking from tiny cups.

Minarets competed for space with church spires, and, at certain times of the day, the Muslim call to prayer battled with the ringing of bells across the river. But the centrepiece of Mostar's old town was definitely its famous bridge.

According to legend, the architect was an Ottoman called Mimar. When Suleiman the Magnificent had commissioned him to build the bridge, Mimar had trembled with fear. He knew the bridge had to span thirty metres, something unimaginable in those days. But that wasn't the source of his angst; it was more to do with the sultan, because, as well as being magnificent, Suleiman was cruel, notorious for his love of gruesome executions. It didn't help that the sultan informed Mimar he would be next in line for the chop if his bridge did not meet the grade.

Mimar began digging his own grave immediately, requesting that the sultan execute him straight away. The sultan refused, and so, reluctantly, Mimar set to work, spending two years on the plans alone. Then, for the next nine years, construction of the bridge went ahead, with protective scaffolding covering the fledgling crossing.

On the day of the grand opening, Mimar fled. He believed the bridge would collapse into the river as soon as the scaffolding was removed. But it didn't, and Mimar returned a hero. His bridge then stood for the next 427 years, until Bosnian Croats destroyed it in 1993.

Reconstructed in 2004, Michael and I stared at the distinctive white, arched crossing, guarded on both sides by stone towers. Below it ran a torrent of green belonging to the Neretva River, its waters swelled by melting snow from the mountains. A tour group stood in the middle of the bridge, right on the hump, listening to their guide. Judging from his accent, they were Italians. He was probably telling them about the Siege of Mostar.

5

Before the war, Mostar's mainly Croat and Muslim population had lived together in relative peace. The Christian Croats mainly resided in the west of the city, the Muslim Bosniaks in the east, but enough of each religion lived in both parts to give it a healthy mix. People crossed freely between the sides, using the old bridge (Stari Most) often, enjoying the cultural diversity of their city.

When war broke out and Serbian forces tried to attack the city, both Croats and Bosniaks joined forces to fight them off. They succeeded, but then started battling among themselves. Croat forces took control of the western side of Mostar and began expelling Muslims, sometimes with violence. Thousands fled to the eastern side of town.

Then the siege began. Croat troops began shelling the eastern part of Mostar in a campaign that lasted eighteen months. Bridges were blown up, mosques attacked, homes and businesses relentlessly shelled. Then, on 9th November 1993, Croat artillery decided to target the famous bridge. According to some news reports, over sixty shells hit the bridge before it collapsed into the river.

The Croats claimed the bridge had been a strategic target, but that was a poor excuse, given that it was a pedestrian-only crossing. Anyway, not long after this event, Muslim forces rallied and took back the city, pushing most of the Croats out.

Today, Bosniaks and Croats (in reduced numbers) still live on their own side of the river. Each has their own schools and services. Relations remain tense between them, but are no longer at dangerous levels. The people of Mostar are simply getting on with their lives.

Michael and I stood on the bridge. The tour group had moved into the old Turkish quarter of the city. It was an area full of stone walls, shuttered windows, rising minarets and cobblestone pathways. We headed there ourselves.

The main street was lined with stalls selling everything from Mostar fridge magnets, brass coffee pots, locally produced handicrafts and Russian dolls, to mementos made from bullet casings. Pens were the most common bullet-themed item for sale, but there were also small tanks and fighter planes, all constructed from spent ammunition. Michael and I decided it was time to get something to eat.

6

"I'm going to have *cevapi*," I said. I'd discounted *fried brain* immediately, and thought that *brizle* sounded too much like something a bird would disgorge. Cevapi was the safest bet.

"Me too," Michael answered.

We were sitting outside, in a busy part of the bazaar. The waiter had told me that cevapi was small grilled sausages stuffed inside pita bread. When the food arrived, I saw that they came with a side portion of raw onion, which I ignored in favour of the meat. It was similar to the meal we'd had in Belgrade at the start of the Odyssey, and was tasty and filling, especially with a nice bottle of Sarajevsko to wash it all down with.

A beggar approached our table, an old woman wearing a shroud of dark layers. I waved her away but she stayed near the table, hand outstretched. To get rid of her, Michael handed her a few coins, and she shuffled off. Almost immediately, another beggar appeared, this one a teenage boy in a dark jacket. Like the woman, his skin was a darker shade than most of the locals, suggesting he was Roma.

He'd clearly seen Michael give the old woman some money, and so he thought he'd chance it too. Michael rolled his eyes and handed the boy a coin, which he took without comment. He walked away.

A short distance from us, I could see a girl aged about six. She was stood with her back to a nearby wall, pretending to cry in order to garner sympathy from passing tourists. As I watched, a woman carrying a baby, presumably the girl's mother, went up to the child. The girl stopped crying straight away. After conferring for a moment, the girl nodded and went off to beg in a more direct manner. She stood in the middle of the cobbles and simply held her hand out. It worked; a tourist couple stopped and handed her some money.

7

Despite the efforts at rebuilding the city, evidence of war was still there to see. Even in the old town, just slightly away from the tourist centre, we saw bullet holes scarring facades above windows.

"Look at that building there," Michael said. He was staring at a line of small shops. Most of them had been renovated, but one had not. Its interior was vacant, its exterior covered in bullet holes. It was a crumbling mess, without any windows or doors, and it gave an indication of just how much Mostar had suffered.

Further along the street was the 16th century Karadzozbey Mosque. It had a tall, spindly minaret and a large round dome. Outside, secured to a fence, was a black-and-white photo of what the mosque had looked like during the war. The dome was caved in, parts of the roof had been shelled to smithereens and the top of the minaret was missing.

Next door was a small cemetery. Prior to the Siege of Mostar, it had been a city park. Each gravestone dated from 1993, and most belonged to Muslim men in their twenties, their birth dates close to mine.

Michael was staring at a small grave adorned with yellow and white flowers. The name of the person was Nersada Maksumim. He had been born in 1993, and had died in 1993. The baby had not even reached his first year.

The worst building we saw was an abandoned supermarket. Bullet holes and large gashes covered the ugly, grey concrete structure where sniper fire and mortar attacks had penetrated it. Steel girders stuck out from its overhanging roof, and even some nearby trees seemed sympathetic to the building's plight: thin and wispy, with barely any green life left within their leaves. A large wire fence surrounded the whole thing, with signs saying: *Attention: Dangerous Ruin. Access forbidden!* There were similar signs all over Mostar.

"Come on," I said to Michael. "Let's head back into the old town."

8

We arrived just in time to see a man about to jump off the old bridge.

Diving off Stari Most was a tradition dating back to the 17th century. Always young men, the reason they did it was to wow the local ladies with their physical prowess and lack of fear. Nowadays, men do it for a much simpler reason: money.

A man wearing a blue wetsuit was limbering himself up on the bridge's hump. His pal was wandering through the crowd with a bucket. People began putting money in, but Mr Bucket deemed the amount too meagre for the jump to go ahead. Another round of money collection began as more people arrived.

The man in the wetsuit was aged about thirty. He was pouring water over himself to cool his skin in preparation for the cold water below. With a sizeable crowd on the bridge, Mr Bucket finally decided that he had collected enough, and gave the signal. The man in the wetsuit nodded and climbed over the fence, facing the river, his arms holding onto the bars.

Everyone waited for the man to dive into the churning green water below, but he simply stood there, puffing his cheeks in and out. Then, with a swift movement, he did it. Instead of diving though, he jumped. Down he plummeted, and then, with an almighty splash, he was in the river, everyone craning their necks to see him. With a bubbling crescendo of applause from the bridge, the man surfaced and waved. We watched as he swam to the side.

9

We decided it was time to climb a minaret. We'd read that the Koski Mehmed Pasha Mosque was open to tourists wanting to see Mostar from a perched position.

The man responsible for the mosque seemed happy to see us, accepting our marks in return for entry tickets. "You do not need to remove shoes," he said, "as long as you keep to green carpet."

We entered the small prayer room, noticing the green carpet. It led to a tiny arched doorway on the right. The narrow, spiralling stone staircase didn't have a handrail, or even a light, and as we made our way up, I grew a little apprehensive. Half way up, I began to have my usual battle over whether I should be climbing to the top. My fear of heights was nowhere near as bad as it had once been, but it still gave me the jitters from time to time.

At its worst, my fear had caused me to walk on my hands and knees around the summit of a small medieval tower in York. My girlfriend at the time had found it immensely embarrassing, but worse were some kids who had pointed and laughed.

I followed Michael up through the minaret, and eventually we came to the top. I didn't dare to look down. Instead I kept my gaze fixed firmly ahead. But what a view! The bridge was flanked on both sides by the gorgeous stone buildings of the old town.

Michael disappeared around the curve of the minaret. Tentatively I followed him, keeping as far back as I could from the edge, even though there was a wall to stop me from toppling over, should I slip.

The view wasn't as good around the other side, so I made a complete circuit back to the start. After one final look at Mostar from above, we headed down the steps, thankful that nobody was coming up. I dreaded to think how they would have passed us.

10

"Do you need a guide?" said a man wearing an identity card around his neck. Michael and I were near the old town again, him taking photos of more bullet-damaged buildings, me standing around waiting.

"No, thanks," I said. It was late in the evening, and we'd seen most of the sights already.

"But I am an official guide," the man pressed, proffering his card. "And I've had my photo taken with Boris Johnson. Perhaps you want to see it?"

Michael walked over to join us, listening in to the conversation.

"No, it's all right," I said. "Anyway, I'm not German." A strange expression crossed the man's face, and he shot Michael a look. "But thanks anyway. Bye."

A few metres away from the guide, Michael turned to me. "Why did you say you were not German?"

"Because he wanted to show me a photo of Boris Johnson."

Michael stared at me quizzically, almost the same look that the guide had given. "So?"

I said, "Why would I want to see a photo of a German tennis player?"

Michael looked bamboozled, but then started laughing. "Because Boris Johnson is not a German tennis player! He's the Mayor of London, you idiot. You're thinking of Boris Becker! The guide must think we're both thick. And he'd be correct about you." Michael laughed again.

"So that's why he looked so confused," I said.

"Exactly."

We found a place to have something to eat. It was off the main street, but still with plenty of passers-by. A middle-aged man on crutches walked past. His right leg was missing below the knee, and, as he struggled along the cobbles, both Michael and I surmised his injury had been caused by the war.

Our food arrived, yet another meat dish swimming in oil, and then two kittens arrived. We nicknamed them the Moustache Cats. One was black and white, the other tabby, both with the same facial markings that cads had favoured in 1930s films. The cats loved the greasy meat, so I was thankful for their presence.

11

I walked up to the hotel barman, a man in his fifties with a black bushy moustache. Michael and I had met him earlier when he'd doubled up as the hotel porter.

"Two Sarajevskos please," I said.

"No problem," he answered retrieving two bottles from the fridge. "Please sit, I bring over."

I did so, joining Michael at a table in the otherwise empty bar. He was leafing through a book he'd found on the reception counter. It was full of photos from the war. He stopped at a photo of the bridge. Only small sections of it remained; the rest had collapsed into the river.

"It was bad," said the barman, placing our drinks on the table, together with a complimentary bowl of crisps, always part of the Bosnian service. "Not a good day."

It was always tricky talking to someone about something horrible. How do you say the right thing? So I nodded at the barman. "Yes, it was."

"For a long time after the war, I tried to forget about what happened. My wife was the same. We never spoke about it."

Michael closed the book and looked up.

"At the start of the war, our first son was born. Croat soldiers were turning up at Muslim houses and taking people away, mostly men. We lived on the eastern side of the river, so were safe from that. But fifteen of my friends on the western side were killed."

I didn't know what to say.

The man looked at us. "But I do not hate the Croats. I just wish they could accept they are Bosnians, like us." He walked off towards the bar.

There was so much I wanted to ask him, but did not dare. Questions such as: *What happened to your son? What was it like living in a city under mortar attack? Did you fight against the Croats? How did you feel when your friends went missing? How did you cope? How did you survive?* We finished our last drinks in Bosnia, and went to our rooms to pack, thoughts spinning in my head.

7. Kotor, Montenegro

Interesting fact: Montenegro translates as Black Mountain.

The drive back to Dubrovnik was straightforward. We dropped the hire car off and planned our trip to Montenegro.

Our first port of call was Dubrovnik Bus Station. We quickly established that a coach left at 3.30pm that afternoon, bound for a place called Herceg Novi. From there, we'd have to reassess the situation. We bought one-way tickets each.

After a quick lunch, we boarded the coach and drove off towards the fifth country of the Odyssey and one of the youngest nations in the world. Montenegro only declared itself independent of Serbia in 2006. Serbia did not object because, mostly, the two entities had been independent in all but name anyway.

South of Dubrovnik, the clouds thickened, and then unleashed a deluge so fierce that it made some cars pull over to the side of the road. Our driver was braver and simply powered through the storm, his windscreen wipers on their most furious setting.

The Montenegro border had a large flag outside. I nodded in appreciation at the design. It was mainly royal red, with a fetching gold border and a yellow two-headed eagle in the middle. It looked like a medieval coat of arms, something a knight might take into battle. Cyrillic was back to prominence again, I noticed, a script we'd not seen in Croatia at all. It was written across the border booth we were waiting at. Formalities were painless: everyone's passport was checked, and the coach moved on.

The road turned east as we traversed the beautiful Bay of Kotor, an inlet of the Mediterranean Sea, but low-level cloud was cloaking the mountains, making them look forbidding. Lashings of rain obscured everything else, including the water.

One and a half hours later, we stopped at the Montenegrin town of Herceg Novi. To ease our arrival, the rain slowed and sunbeams broke through gaps in the grey. As we collected our bags, the rain stopped altogether.

2

Despite not knowing anything about Herceg Novi, we were delighted to discover it was a great little town. It had a central area full of bars and cafes, a medieval gateway with turrets and a little castle sat on top of a hill.

Montenegrins seemed a friendly lot. As Michael and I wandered through the old town gateway, people stood chatting to one another or waving across the street at someone they recognised. Everybody seemed to know each other, and the old town was full of laughter and chatter.

We found ourselves in a pretty square with a church at its centre. Suddenly, the sound of a piano playing a classical piece floated along the cobbles into our ears. It made us curious. We followed the source of the music until we came to the end of a narrow street. The pianist was playing inside a large building with green-shuttered windows. A big sign on the front read: Muzicka Skola, *Music School*.

We found a cheap restaurant in the old town and had a quick drink. Then it was back to the bus station to buy tickets for our onwards connection to Kotor, another UNESCO World Heritage site. The Balkans was full of them.

3

Kotor reminded me of a small Dubrovnik. It had the same orange terracotta roofs crammed higgledy-piggledy inside an old city wall. Some dramatic mountains towered over one side of the town. Half way up them was a fort we would visit the next day. On the other side was the Bay of Kotor. Now that the rain had disappeared, we could see just how beautiful the scenery was.

After depositing our bags in the small hotel, Michael and I found a cafe in a large square near the stone entrance gate. It was called the Square of Arms because, at one point, the town's arsenal had been kept there. A Michael Bolton tune wafted over us while we waited for our drinks to arrive.

"What is it with Michael Bolton?" I asked, shaking my head. On the coach from Herceg Novi, a CD featuring the American crooner had played throughout. He seemed the most popular musician in the country.

Almost everyone around us was smoking. Everybody in the Balkans seemed to smoke, and could do it where they liked. After finishing our drinks, we left Michael Bolton to his cigarette-friendly audience and found a little pizzeria. After a nice meal, we headed back to the hotel. It had been a long day.

4

The streets of Kotor's old town were narrow, but full of colour. It was the next morning, and we were passing ornate wooden doorways, stone archways, and old-fashioned bicycles left against lampposts. Above us, lines of washing dangled in the breeze, and there was always something interesting to catch our eyes. But one type of establishment that seemed at odds with Kotor's quaintness was its casinos. Michael and I were walking along a pretty side street, watching out for the uneven cobbles, when we passed one. It was called the Automat Club, and had a large placard near the door that showed a girl draped over a roulette table. We walked past it, heading uphill, until we arrived at the start of the trail.

"Ready?" Michael said with relish.

"I think so..."

The strenuous stretch of 1350 loose steps led up to Saint John's fortress. It offered the best views of Kotor, the guidebook said. It also stressed that only people who were physically fit should attempt the climb. I doubted very much whether I belonged in that category.

And so we began.

5

After a hundred metres or so, we arrived at a gate with an ominous sign attached to it: *Entrance to the Fortress. Caution: Risk Zone!* We stopped, regarded it, but then, like warriors, stepped past it.

"This isn't so bad," I said, a quarter of the way up. The steps were loose in certain places, but mostly they were okay, and, with the sun shining overhead, I was quite enjoying myself.

Michael stopped to take a photo of the view. The blue-green water of Kotor Bay stretched off until it met the mountains in the distance. We could also see the triangular layout of the old town, as well as its small harbour with a few yachts moored by the edge.

A group of teenage boys were coming down from the opposite direction. All three had dark hair, like most Montenegrins, but they also had a dog with them, a Golden Labrador.

Because we were ascending a particularly steep section of the trail, my pulse was racing and my breathing short, but, as we neared the boys, I held my breath, so they would not know how tired I was. Michael had already passed them, displaying a level of fitness I never knew he possessed. The boys smiled and said something to me, but I couldn't understand what, so simply nodded. As they passed, I noticed one boy had a plastic bag filled with empty lager cans. They had clearly been having a few sneaky beers at the top of the hill. But at least they were environmentally conscious enough to bring their empties back down with them.

"Come on," Michael shouted a few minutes later. He was waiting for me, clearly itching to get to the top so he could take more photographs.

"Why don't you ever delete any?" I asked when I'd caught him up. Michael had once told me that his home computer was bursting with every photo he'd ever taken. He never deleted any, not even blurry or half-formed ones.

"Because I don't need to. When I run out of hard drive space – which will be never – then I might think about it."

I pondered this. I enjoyed, and appreciated, good photography, but was diligent about deleting ones that looked wrong or boring. That way, I could look back on a few select photos and enjoy them. There was no way Michael could do that. It would take him days to flick through his endless collection.

"Look!" I said, picking up a fragment of rock from the ground. "It's a piece of flint from the bronze age. Some sort of tool, I think. It should be in a museum. Why don't you take a photo?"

Michael looked at the rock, and then at me. "Because a flint tool would not be from the Bronze Age. I think you mean the Stone Age. And, secondly, it's just a piece of rock."

"I know. But museums are full of stuff like this." I turned the flat piece of grey stone over in my hand. "I reckon I could open a museum and put this in a glass cabinet. It would have a caption saying: *Flint arrowhead from the Stone Age*, and people like you would take photos of it. Except I wouldn't let you. Strictly no photography in the *Museum of Old Shite*."

I stood up and forced myself forward.

Thirty minutes later, we arrived at the summit. There was a collection of stone ruins and a huge Montenegrin flag flapping in the mountain breeze. We had the whole place to ourselves. I actually felt a sense of accomplishment at reaching the top. I had proven to myself that I wasn't such a lazy lump after all.

6

We were back in the old town, wondering what to do about food. The pizzerias and cafes all looked nice, but their prices were similar to Dubrovnik's, and we needed to be careful with money from now on. We still had three more countries to go before we flew home.

We decided the best bet would be to buy some provisions from a supermarket. We found one just outside the old town, past the yacht marina. The marina had expensive vessels from as far away as Malta, Russia, and, strangely, Delaware.

The supermarket was guarded by a set of drunkards. All three had scraggly beards and huge bottles of cheap beer. They didn't seem to be in a gang or anything, but obviously congregated there for company. One man sat underneath a lamppost, smiling to himself, hand curled around his prized bottle of Jelen Pivo – a super-sized plastic container with 2 litres of the stuff inside. Another man stood by the door, doing nothing in particular. The third man was the most animated. He was standing away from the entrance, half on the pavement and half on the road. He was arguing with an invisible adversary, staggering backwards and forwards, making exaggerated arm movements and unintelligible noises. Michael and I sidestepped the gauntlet of grogginess and entered the supermarket.

Ten minutes later, we came out with some bread, cheese, Snickers bars, and a slag. "I'm having it first," I announced. "I don't want your sloppy seconds." Two of the drunkards were still hanging around, but the third one, the fighter, was gone.

"Fine. Just make sure you leave enough for me."

Slag was a brand of Montenegrin ice-cream, and as soon as we found a bench, I got Michael to take a photo of me holding the tub. I posted it on Facebook with a caption that read: *Jason enjoying some Montenegrin slag*. When I checked in later, someone had commented. *She's not a proper slag because she's still got her top on.*

After Michael had sampled some slag, we discarded the container, and sought out a cafe with free Wi-Fi. We had to get to Tirana the next day and needed to find out how to go about it.

7

There were no buses from Kotor to Tirana; it was as simple as that. No amount of web searching revealed otherwise. Compounding matters was that I'd already emailed my contact in Albania, a man with the unlikely name of Elton. I'd arranged for him to pick us up three days hence. Elton was going to drive us to Macedonia. Therefore, we had to get to Tirana the next day. If we failed to do so, it wouldn't leave us enough time to see the city. But without a bus, we were stuck.

"Stop fretting," Michael said, taking a sip of lager. "There'll be a way. Tomorrow morning we'll go to the bus station, and find out about transport to Albania. There'll be something."

"Why don't we go to the bus station now? That way we can find out for sure. Otherwise I won't be able to relax all evening."

The bus station was just behind the supermarket, and, thankfully, we found a man who spoke some English.

"You must get bus to Ulcinj," he told us, pointing to a map on his wall. Ulcinj was a Montenegrin costal town near the Albanian border. "When you arrive at bus station, you may take taxi to border. It not far. Then on Albania side, get minibus to Tirana. Very easy. Many people do this every day."

I asked him about luggage. After all, Michael and I had large backpacks each.

"No problem," said the man. "Very easy. Tomorrow you come here and buy ticket for Ulcinj. It leave at twelve fifteen pm. Be here early to get ticket please."

We thanked him and wandered back to the old town to get something to eat. Tomorrow was going to be a strange day, I reckoned, fraught with unknowns. But at least we had a plan.

So Michael and I packed our bags for yet another journey through the Balkans. Already in the Odyssey, we'd stayed in six different places, all in less than two weeks. But out of all the places on the list, Albania was the one I was most looking forward to.

Albania had always appealed to me. Perhaps its communist past drew me, or maybe its relative isolation within Europe. Whatever the reason, I was excited.

8. Tirana, Albania

Interesting fact: There are still over 700,000 concrete bunkers littering Albania.

Getting to the Albania border was as straightforward as the man in the bus station had said it would be. Ulcinj turned out to be another deliciously pretty coastal town, but all Michael and I saw of it was a cafe in the bus station. With a goal of reaching Tirana before nightfall, we decided to get straight on with the journey. After a quick cup of coffee, we jumped in a taxi to take us the short distance to the border.

Once stamped into the poorest nation of the Balkans, we considered our options. There were a few minivans waiting nearby, as well as three taxis.

"How much to Tirana?" I asked the first taxi driver.

"Two hundred euro," the Albanian cab driver answered, looking at me, and then Michael, who was standing a short distance away with our bags.

I scoffed at his price, and went to the next driver. He was standing against his car with a folded-up newspaper in his hand.

"Two hundred euro," he said, as well. It appeared that the price to Tirana was fixed.

I felt a knot in my stomach. Two hundred euros was far too much. I decided to try driver number three; this one was sitting in his car, but he said two hundred as well.

"One hundred," I said, hoping for the best.

The taxi driver shook his head and flicked the end of his cigarette out of the window. "No."

"One hundred and fifty?" I suggested.

The man looked up, considering it. "One hundred and seventy euro."

Well, at least it was heading in the right direction. "Hang on," I said, and rushed over to Michael. His face flinched when I told him the price. "I vote for trying one of the minibuses," he said.

I wandered over to one of the old-looking vans, and saw that there was no driver. Instead, I looked at the front of the van, but didn't recognise any of the words, let alone any possible destinations. I'd been hoping it would say Tirana on the front.

A few passengers were sitting inside, waiting for it to fill up. I put my head through the door and addressed them. "Is this bus going to Tirana?"

Everyone looked at me, but no one answered.

"Tirana?" I asked again, hoping for a more positive response. Still no one spoke.

Bugger this, I said to myself, and returned to Michael. "Taxi it is, then," he said.

2

The drive to the Albanian capital took just over two hours, but, for most of the journey, I kept my eyes closed, weary with the stress of travel and movement. At one point, when I opened them, I saw fields being tended to by men and women with hoes. Children helped by shovelling hay. In contrast, billboards advertised the latest mobile phone companies.

As we reached the city centre, cars clogged the streets. When the traffic eventually got going, every driver seemed to take great delight in ignoring all traffic signals. Roundabouts were a free-for-all, and the two-lane highway that led through the centre of Tirana was like a scene from the *Wacky Races*. Cars were driving four abreast, many of them beeping and swerving as if they were in a Death Race. I'd not seen traffic like this since Cairo. Mercedes-Benz cars seemed the vehicle of choice, but judging by the state of them, most had seen better days.

Construction was going on everywhere, with piles of building materials left by the side of many roads. I'd read that rapid, and often unregulated, construction, coupled with the 1980s fume-belching vehicles, was causing appalling pollution in the Albanian capital. But it didn't seem that bad to me as we jolted along the street.

"Where you want to go?" asked the taxi driver. He'd been mute for nearly the entire journey, no doubt in response to Michael reading and me napping.

"Hotel Nobel," I said. "On Boulevard Zogu 1." We'd booked the cheap hotel when we'd found some free Wi-Fi in Kotor.

The driver said nothing, but seemed to understand where we wanted to go. A few minutes later, he pulled up outside a small establishment. The Hotel Nobel was right in the centre of the city.

"Well, thank God for that," I said. We paid the driver and then checked in. The twin beds in our room were to our satisfaction, and, now that our plans were back on track, I could finally relax. We had the whole of the next day to see what Tirana was like; the day after, Elton, my Albanian contact, would pick us up at 8am. We decided to celebrate by going for a beer.

3

The evening streets of Tirana were full of people sauntering by, or sitting in outdoor bars and cafes. Michael and I walked to Skanderbeg Square, the focal point of the city, marvelling at the tastefully-lit buildings that lined the whole area.

In the middle of the square was a pedestrian-only island housing a large statue of Albanian hero, Skanderbeg, for whom the square was named. Back in the 15th century, he'd made his name by repelling an Ottoman invasion. The warrior was sitting on a horse at the top of a large stone plinth. He was wearing a strange-looking hat that looked like a cross between a Viking helmet and something a court jester would wear. But with the seriously pointy sword in his hand, and a scary beard on his face, I would not have argued with him about it.

Skanderbeg Square was expansive, with a range of notable buildings, including the Et'Hem Bey Mosque, the Tirana International Hotel, a huge opera house (that was part of the enormous Palace of Culture) and the distinctive National History Museum, with its famous mosaic on the front. We would visit more of them the next day, but for now, we simply stared about, taking everything in while the sun went down.

Skanderbeg Square had once looked different. When Albania had possessed a royal family, the centre of the square featured a large fountain. And where the Palace of Culture stood, there had been a colourful bazaar. Before the construction of the hotel, there had been an Orthodox Cathedral. Almost every original building from the square had been demolished to make way for the new ones.

Still, I liked Skanderbeg Square. Maybe it was because evening had fallen, masking the grime, or maybe it was the minarets offering their calls to prayer. Whatever the reason, I was glad to be there.

Michael and I found a bar. A couple of bottles of Beer Tirana came with a price tag of only 370 lek (£2.20), and, like other places in the Balkans, the drinks came with a complimentary bowl of crisps. Albania was impressing me a lot.

4

The next morning was hot and sunny, and, after a five-course breakfast courtesy of the Hotel Nobel (the final course was a plate of sliced banana), we were off to see the sights. First port of call was a small outdoor market, which, according to the guidebook, was a must-see sight.

"It's not that good," Michael said as we strolled past stalls specialising in fruit and vegetables. Further along, stalls sold fish, which in the heat were beginning to smell. Suddenly, something caught my eye. It was a line of cooked sheep heads slowly rotating on a skewer. They looked gruesome and mesmerising at the same time.

To get back to the main square we had to pass through a small park littered with benches. Each bench contained two or three old men, most of whom were wearing trilby hats. The men were obviously enjoying hanging out together, patting each other on the backs after hearty guffaws. The men, no doubt, were old enough to recall a time when things were not so easy in Tirana.

5

Despite the capital's outward show of prosperity, Albania is actually one of Europe's poorest countries, with only Ukraine and Moldova coming out in worse shape. Its misfortune lay in the legacy left over from ex-ruler Enver Hoxha, or Supreme Comrade, as he liked to call himself.

In the 1940s, Albania had embraced communism. Hoxha abolished the monarchy, eliminated political opponents and achieved total control by using imprisonment and execution as a matter of course.

Despite having similar ideologies with Yugoslavia, Hoxha quickly fell out with Josip Tito, and instead made friends with the Soviets. When Stalin died, he switched allegiance to the Chinese, especially when they sent him billions of dollars in aid. The Soviets later described Hoxha as being 'like a dog that bites the hand who feeds it'.

Clerical workers were sent to the fields, and religion was banned, but, despite this, at least at first, Albania did okay. The State University of Tirana was set up in 1957, and, at the same time, literacy levels soared. The country became agriculturally self-sufficient, and with the economy doing well (thanks largely to

Chinese input), Albania became the only country in the world, at that time, not to tax its citizens.

However, not all was good. Behind the scenes, Hoxha was growing paranoid, especially when it came to the Soviets. He believed they were plotting to invade his country and remove him from power. Then, as relations with China deteriorated, due in part to Richard Nixon's visit to Beijing, the economy slowed. By 1978, the Chinese had had enough of Hoxha and pulled the plug. The Albanian economy crumbled.

Holing himself up in Tirana, Hoxha ordered the construction of three quarters of a million igloo-shaped concrete bunkers to protect his borders. The amount of money spent on them was staggering and compounded the financial woes of the nation. With no friends at all, Albania became an isolated state, cut off from the outside world. But this gave Hoxha an opportunity to develop his own strange cult of personality.

He had statues made of himself and set them up all over Tirana. He also developed a persona whereby his citizens thought him a genius, capable of making decisions on any part of their lives. It was around this time that Hoxha became known as *Great Teacher*.

To stop any unrest that may have been brewing, Hoxha imprisoned thousands of citizens whom he accused of being *enemies of the people*. Foreign travel was banned for everyone (except for strictly controlled business trips), as were beards. The latter was for two reasons: one to curtail any Islamic tendencies, the other simply that Hoxha thought them unhygienic.

By now, Albania was on its knees, with the lowest standard of living across Europe. Hoxha's version of isolationist communism had been a catastrophic failure. To the world at large, Albania was a failed state, a backwards nation with no prospects, and a joke.

Enver Hoxha eventually died in 1985, leaving a country desperate and alone. His communist party managed to cling to power until 1992, when a democratic government ousted them. Finally, Albania opened up to the world.

6

The National History Museum dominated one edge of Skanderbeg Square, a building photographed often because of the huge and colourful mosaic on its front. The mosaic depicted proud Albanians marching through history.

I knew Michael would want to go in, because we hadn't visited a museum for a few days. In fact, the last one had been in Dubrovnik. Back in Kotor, he'd wanted to visit the Maritime Museum, but I managed to convince him that, if we did, we would not have enough time to climb to the fort. But that was two days ago, and so, when Michael said he wanted to go in the National History Museum, I couldn't really refuse.

But fortune was smiling on my side, because the huge museum was closed, as it was every Monday. "Oh well," I said, reading the opening times. "What a shame."

Michael glared at me, but said nothing. We looked around and noticed the 18th century Et'hem Bey Mosque at the other side of the square. During Enver Hoxha's rule, his communist officials had closed it down. Next door to it was a tall clock tower that we reckoned we could climb. We crossed the square to find out.

Once there, Michael and I found a man inside the clock tower who said we could climb it, for the reasonable price of 100 lek (60p) each. We paid and began the slog up the ninety spiralling steps.

The ascent was certainly easier than the dark minaret of Mostar. At the top, a small viewing platform offered a panoramic view across Skanderbeg Square and beyond. Just next to us was a tall minaret, its loudspeakers pointing downwards towards the pavements.

Around the other side of the platform, we could see the colourful buildings of downtown Tirana. The city was famous for its colourful buildings - bright yellows, greens and pinks - all giving the ageing concrete apartment blocks a splash of personality and verve. The ex-Mayor of Tirana, Edi Rama, had come up with the idea.

"The buildings look nice," admitted Michael after he'd fired off about a dozen photographs. "But it's superficial. All it's done is paper over the cracks. Instead of sorting out the problems of power and water, all the mayor did was to pick up a paintbrush."

I looked down at the work of a mayor-cum-artist. Even if he had only glossed over some of Tirana's issues, it certainly beat bare concrete any day.

7

At the bottom of the clock tower we found some steps to sit on to ponder our next move. An old man was sitting nearby, playing a flute-like instrument. He had a hat between his feet, spattered with a few coins.

"There's meant to be some sort of fortress around here somewhere," I said, after studying the map. Michael needed no further prompting and grabbed it from my hand.

"Come on then," he said excitedly, just as I knew he would. He was standing up, rotating his head in the direction of travel. Anything with the word *ruin* or *fort* in it would make him grow animated.

"Up here!" he said a few minutes later, as we negotiated some sort of building site. It was a shortcut, Michael insisted. We passed a vacant digger sitting in the mud and then came to something quite unexpected. It was a set of old Soviet-era monuments left to gather dust behind a nondescript building. Michael stopped and looked at the map, then at the guidebook index, but found no mention of what we had stumbled across.

The largest statues were of Lenin and Stalin, with Lenin, in particular, looking in a sorry state of repair. He had gaping holes all over his metalwork. Stalin was in better condition, but numerous bird droppings signified he had not been cleaned in a while. Next to them was an abandoned car with four flat tyres.

"This is a rare find," said Michael, pointing at Stalin, who was double my height. The old Soviet leader was wearing a long trench coat and sporting his distinctive thick moustache and cap. "There are not many of these left." After posing for some photos, we moved on to resume our search of the ruins.

We found them a few minutes later, but all that remained were a few sections of old wall, mostly incorporated into a newer building. Had we not known the ruins of a 6th century Byzantine settlement were there, we would've walked right past without even noticing their presence.

"Well, that wasn't worth the effort," I remarked. And for once, Michael seemed to agree, not even bothering with his camera.

8

Before Enver Hoxha had established his communist state, the comical-sounding King Zog (real name: Ahmed BeyZogu) ruled Albania. Prior to becoming king, however, Zog had simply been the President of Albania. But that all changed in 1928, when he decided to have a crown and a throne made. When they were finished, he promptly declared himself King Zog I.

One of the first things he did was to invent a brand new salute (right hand, palm down, stretching straight across the chest towards the heart), and cemented his authority by hoarding the nation's gold.

Zog also broke off his engagement to the new Prime Minister's daughter, which angered the politician. And this was when blood vengeance (a tradition in Albania whereby a wronged person had the right to kill a wrongdoer) was still popular. The new king became so paranoid that he appointed a platoon of personal guards to accompany him wherever he went, and had his mother (now known as the Queen Mother of Albania) supervise the Royal Kitchens in case one of his chefs tried to poison him.

But it seemed his paranoia was well founded, because, during his reign, King Zog endured 55 assassination attempts, the most memorable of which occurred in Vienna in 1931.

Zog had been to the opera, and was about to get into his car when someone took a shot at him. Unlike most rulers, who might have hidden behind a set of bodyguards, Zog sprang into immediate action. He whipped his own pistol out, and fired back, which sent his assailant scarpering. Because of this bizarre event, Zog made history. He became the only modern Head of State to ever exchange gunfire with a potential assassin.

Despite his heroics, Zog's eventual downfall occurred when Italian troops invaded Albania, forcing him to flee to England. He took with him all the gold plundered from the treasury and rented a whole floor of London's Ritz Hotel. After a brief foray into America (where he attempted to smuggle in his entire entourage), he settled in the French Riviera, living a life of luxury until his death, aged 65. Perhaps as a memorial to the man's colourful past, the Albanian authorities eventually named a street after the exiled monarch, appropriately called Boulevard Zog I. Our hotel was located just off it.

9

"Shall we find Hoxha's Pyramid?" Michael suggested after lunch. I nodded. I'd already mentioned I wanted to see the strange structure built after the ex-leader's death. From what I'd read, it was a cross between an Aztec pyramid and a concrete spaceship.

Built in 1988, three years after Hoxha's death, the massive concrete and glass building was initially used as a museum dedicated to his life. After the fall of communism, all of Hoxha's memorabilia was removed and the pyramid changed into a cultural centre. This lasted for a few years. Then the building went into decline, and the government removed all the marble slabs, leaving only bare concrete behind. And that was how it remains to this day.

We found Hoxha's Pyramid in a small park south of Skanderbeg Square. As we trailed through the grass leading to the oddity, it seemed that every graffiti artist in Tirana had left their mark somewhere on it, giving Hoxha's Pyramid an even deeper sense of abandonment.

"They're thinking of pulling it down," Michael told me as we stood on the steps that led to the now derelict pyramid. To me, it wasn't so much a pyramid; it was more like a squashed packing box with a vague pyramid feel. "They want to replace it with a nice shiny parliament building."

I stared up the thing, wondering whether this would be for the best. After all, it looked a wreck, an eyesore even. On the other hand, perhaps that was why it was so fascinating. I mentioned this to Michael.

He agreed. "Yeah, it's one of those things that, on paper, should be a crime against taste – a diabolical thing – but when you actually see it, you can't take your eyes off it. I think it would be a shame if they demolished it."

Apparently, it was possible (though probably illegal) to clamber up the sides of the pyramid in order to get a great view of the city. As we walked up the cracked, graffiti covered steps to reach the entrance, we wondered whether to give it a go. From a distance, the roof gradient had looked slight, but now, up close and personal, it looked trickier.

"What do you think?" I asked.

"I'm not sure."

We decided against scaling the monstrosity, and instead peered into the darkened interior. We found a gap in some wooden slats and looked in. From what we could make out, the inside was a bare shell, filled with the odd cement mixer. We left the landmark and headed further south towards Mother Teresa Square.

10

Mother Teresa only visited Albania once. In fact, the great lady had been born in Skopje, in neighbouring Macedonia. However, because her mother had been an ethnic Albanian, the nation had claimed the saintly woman as their own, naming the international airport after her and having a public holiday dedicated to her.

Mother Teresa Square was a dull part of the city, dominated at one end by the University of Tirana. A few students were milling about outside, some of them with piles of books in their arms. We stopped at a statue of Mother Teresa and then looked at the map.

Michael told me that something called The Grand Park was just behind us. "It's got a lake in it, and some monuments. Fancy it?"

I couldn't think of anything better, so nodded. Besides, it would be nice to get away from the dust and honking of downtown Tirana. My initial impression of the city's smog problem had been wrong. Smoke and dust *were* everywhere in Tirana. Pollution-belching old vehicles, burning piles of rubbish, and environmentally-lacking construction works were all playing their part. Soot covered many buildings and, occasionally, the air was so oppressive that I had to hold my breath. Sazan Guri, an Albanian ecologist, had once joked, 'The dust in Tirana has some air in it.' He was not wrong.

We found the entrance to the park a short distance away. We picked a trail and started our walk. A minute later, we saw what appeared to be a naked man.

He was lying in the grass, a short distance away from the trail, his large potbelly facing the sun. The only item covering his dignity was a pair of old underpants. For a moment, we wondered whether he was dead, but then we saw he was smoking. He coughed, which caused his massive stomach to quiver and roll.

"Does he realise what he looks like?" I asked Michael quietly.

"I don't know. But there's another."

The second man was lying in the grass some distance away from the first man. Like him, he was in the same state of undress, lying on his back, enjoying the sun from his position in the grass. He had sunglasses on and had a bottle of beer next to him.

Michael shook his head, as nonplussed as I was.

And then we spotted a third man, then a fourth. The Grand Park was full of naked men.

11

"Where the hell are we?" I asked. It was twenty minutes later, and I was getting sick and tired of traipsing along dirt paths filled with tiny lizards. My feet were hurting and I needed a drink. The only consolation was that we'd not seen any naked men for a while; in fact, we hadn't seen anyone.

"We're heading north," Michael answered pedantically. Then he sneezed because of the hay fever that had gripped him. We both trudged onwards for a few minutes until we emerged from the woods. There was a road in front of us, crossing right to left. As we stood by the verge wondering whether to cross over, we heard car engines.

We stepped back into the tree line, just as a cavalcade of vehicles sped past, a set of black cars flashing their lights. They followed the road downhill, and then rounded a bend where they disappeared from sight. We wondered who they were, and where they were going, and so, after some deliberation, we decided to follow the road, especially since it offered respite from trampling through the forest.

Around the curve, we saw a guard post and barrier. Beyond them was the rest of the road, and then more forest. The cars were gone, but there was a guard staring at us. He was standing outside a hut. We stopped some distance away so that Michael could get his bearings. He sneezed again.

"Okay..." said Michael, "I think I know where we are. We're near the Palace of the Brigades, where King Zog used to live. It's now the official residence of the current president. We won't be able to see it though; it's surrounded by trees."

I had a look around, trying to find gaps in the foliage, but Michael was correct; there was nothing to see. The guard was still staring, though, perhaps wondering whether we were a threat to the country.

"The lake is around here somewhere," said Michael, unconcerned that an armed sentry was looking at us. "But it's not on the map. Why don't you ask the guard where it is?"

"Why don't you ask him?" I retorted.

"I asked first, and, besides, I've got hay fever. I don't want to sneeze over an Albanian soldier."

With a sigh, I wandered over to the guard post. There was not one guard, but two. One was sitting inside the booth, reading a newspaper.

"Hello," I said to the young man outside. "Do you speak English?"

The guard nodded.

"We are looking for the lake. Do you know where it is?"

The guard raised his eyebrows. "What you look for?"

"The lake. Water. You know..." I mimed rowing a boat.

The guard nodded in understanding. "Wait," he said, and stepped back inside the booth. After some consultation with his colleague, he came out and pointed up the hill, back the way we had come. "Up and then turn right. Not left! I repeat, not left!"

I thanked him and returned to Michael.

12

The guard watched as we made our way up the hill. I knew this because I kept turning around to check. At the other side of the hill, there was a fork in the road. I turned to Michael, who was busy sneezing and rubbing his eyes. "Did the guard say left...or was it right?"

Michael looked at me, eyes streaming. "I don't know. You spoke to him."

We headed left.

The new path bisected a thick wooded area. We continued along it until we came to a sign that read: *Military Zone*. Michael and I stopped and looked at each other. A second later, we scarpered the hell away, Michael wheezing, as we crunched through the undergrowth like a couple of crazed elephants.

We eventually found the lake, and found a few bathers taking advantage of the good weather. They were all splashing around at the water's edge. All of them were semi-naked men.

"Shall we get naked and join them?" I joked.

Michael thought for a second. "Why not! And we can take photos to post on Facebook."

We headed away from the park and back into the city centre.

13

"I've noticed something about the women in Tirana," I said to Michael as we sat enjoying a Beer Tirana in a city centre bar later that evening. "The young ones are all gorgeous and slim, but then something odd happens."

I was referring to a trait I'd noticed elsewhere in Eastern Europe. When certain girls reached a particular age, a high proportion of them did one of two things, with many doing both: one, they cut their hair quite short and dyed it a strange dark-red colour, and two, they altered their physique so that they morphed into the shape of a Romanian shot putter. I told Michael this.

"A massive over-generalization," he said, quite rightly. "I've seen lots of slim, older women with normal hair." As he said this, a large lady with ruby hair wandered past carrying a couple of bags of turnips.

We relocated to the 18th floor of the Sky Club Bar. We found some outdoor seats and marvelled at the views. We could see right across the city, with some brooding mountains in the distance. Down below, we could still hear the orchestral trumpeting of car horns, but at least the air was clearer. With a cool breeze flowing across us, Michael and I both agreed that we had found the best place to sit in Tirana.

"What's your verdict, then?" I asked. I was gazing at the mountains fading into the shadows behind the city limits.

"I've enjoyed it. It's friendly, it's cheap, it has lots of things to see, and I think more people should visit. How about you?"

"I've wanted to come to Albania for a long time. I know it's not as pretty as Dubrovnik, and doesn't have the history of places like Mostar or Belgrade, but it does have *something*. I like it."

"May I join you?" said a woman's voice. Michael and I turned to see a forty-something lady with a smouldering cigarette in her hand. Her accent suggested she was German. "I overheard you speaking English, and presumed you are tourists, like me. Am I correct?"

We nodded and made a space for the woman to sit down. She was called Amelia and told us she was from Vienna.

"I drove here two days ago, by myself. I've always wanted to come back to Tirana because I was a student here many years ago. I can't believe how much it has changed!"

She lit another cigarette. "I know the Vice-Prime Minister of Albania. I knew him when he was a student in Vienna, and helped him find somewhere to stay. And now he has repaid the favour to me. I met him yesterday. But only for short while because he is so busy."

After chatting about her drive over from Vienna, and that we had probably missed each other at the border town of Ulcinj by only a few hours, we said farewell to Amelia. We had to head back to the Hotel Nobel to pack. Elton, my Albanian contact, was picking us up the next morning for the drive to Macedonia.

Michael and I were now on the final furlong of our Balkan Odyssey.

9. Ohrid, Macedonia

Interesting fact: The average Macedonian eats 120 eggs per year. Americans eat half that.

We finally met Elton the next morning. He was in his late-twenties, with black hair and a thin goatee beard. He bore an uncanny resemblance to a young Graham Norton.

Elton spotted us immediately because Michael and I were the only people standing in the Hotel Noble's small foyer with large bags.

"Jason?" he asked in a thick accent.

I smiled and nodded. "Yes. And this is Michael." We all shook hands.

Elton's tour company was the only one to reply to my email correspondence. I'd emailed a few businesses, asking whether it was possible for them to drive us to Skopje, with a stopover in Ohrid. Ohrid was a reportedly beautiful lakeside town just across the border from Albania. Elton had replied saying his company could do it, and quoted a reasonable price. I later learned that his travel company consisted of just one person – Elton.

As we walked to Elton's car in the morning sunshine, he told us that his girlfriend would be coming with us too. "I hope this is okay...? But it is such a long drive to Skopje and back that she thought it better to keep me company."

His girlfriend, Kaltrina, was a pretty, dark-haired woman who could speak English, but preferred to let Elton do most of the talking. As we set off, Elton told us that the previous week he had been a guide for a couple of journalists. "They were from the *Lonely Planet* magazine and were doing a feature on Albania. Their article will be published in a few months, I think."

Unlike most of his fellow countrymen, Elton was a safe driver. "Most accidents in Albania are caused by stupid driving," he told us. "People overtake when they shouldn't, or they do not take notice of signs. But I blame the Italians and Greeks. They were the ones who taught us how to drive, and they were not the best teachers."

As the outskirts of Tirana faded, we began a gradual climb into the mountains. The scenery was breathtaking, and the hairpin bends exciting. I asked Elton if we would see any of Hoxha's famous bunkers along the way.

He laughed. "Everyone wants to see the bunkers. And yes, you will see lots. Maybe one day I will open a bunker hotel! I will be rich!"

"Are any bunkers for sale?" I asked, intrigued at the idea.

Elton snorted. "No, but the land they sit on is for sale. You buy the land, and the bunker comes free."

Kaltrina spoke up. "Most of the bunkers have been abandoned, but some are cafes or shelters for the animals. Some homeless people, I think, live in them."

Apparently, there was one concrete bunker for every four citizens of Albania, Elton informed us, and the cost of producing three quarters of a million of them had been staggering, causing a massive drain on the country's resources. "He did not care that roads needed repairing, or that people needed houses. All Hoxha was interested in was protecting the borders."

Hoxha's engineers had built bunkers on beaches, on hills, in fields, and in the middle of busy streets. Famously, they even constructed one on the lawn of Albania's best hotel. Graveyards didn't escape Hoxha's *bunkerisation* either. Nowhere was sacred from them.

Such was Hoxha's paranoia about an invasion that he trained a quarter of Albania's population to use the bunkers as defensive structures. At school, from the age of three, teachers taught children to be 'vigilant for the enemy'.

When one of Hoxha's military advisors pointed out that, although the bunkers were undoubtedly strong, a regular, well-equipped army would be more useful in repelling foreign invaders, he was arrested. He was charged with being an agent of the Chinese and executed.

Elton checked his watch. "If it's okay with you," he said, "we can stop in the next town for a drink?"

I looked at Michael, who shrugged. "Fine with us," he said.

2

Elbasan was a large town in the middle of Albania. Oddly enough, one of its sister cities was Newcastle upon Tyne. We parked near Elbasan Castle, a 15th century fortress built by the Ottomans. It had high stone walls, a few round towers, and a tall clock tower. We followed Elton and Kaltrina through the entrance to a cafe.

The four of us sat down around an outdoor table and, when our drinks arrived, I asked our Albanian friends how long they had been together as a couple.

Kaltrina looked at me but said nothing, waiting for Elton to come up with the correct answer.

"About two and a half years," he said, eyes flicking to his girlfriend for confirmation. She nodded. He'd passed the test.

"Any wedding plans?" asked Michael, causing both Elton and Kaltrina to look coy for a second or two.

"You know what?" Elton said eventually. "I am waiting until she deserves me." This comment earned him a swift nudge in the ribs.

Kaltrina addressed us. "In Albania, a bride will not buy a wedding dress like in other countries. Instead, she will rent it. There is big business in Tirana for wedding dress shops."

Elton nodded. "Wedding dress shops are everywhere in Albania. The owners will buy an expensive dress, for maybe two thousand euros, and then rent it out. After a couple of months, the dress will pay for itself."

We finished our drinks and headed back to the car.

3

A few kilometres from the Macedonian border, Elton stopped and pointed out a bunker. It was in a field, a short distance from the road. It looked just like a concrete igloo.

"Go and see it," Elton suggested. "It is safe, don't worry."

Michael and I got out, leaving Elton and Kaltrina in the car. Kaltrina was already reading a magazine, with no interest at all in the bunker.

We crossed the field towards the concrete bastion. It was exactly as I hoped it would be – all bunker-like and totally ridiculous. It wasn't that big, maybe capable of holding two or three people, but it definitely looked sturdy. Its entrance was blocked by a few pieces of wood, as was the thin observation gap. Around its base, people had sprayed or scrawled graffiti.

"Look," said Michael.

In the hills surrounding us, were about twenty or thirty other bunkers, mostly smaller ones, all facing the same general direction. They were everywhere, the folly of a dictator putting his obsession before the needs of his people.

After taking a few photos, we headed back to the car.

4

"Have either of you ever been to Corfu?" asked Elton. We were passing even more bunkers in an area of Albania seemingly bonkers for bunkers.

I hadn't and nor had Michael.

"Well, in certain places, Corfu is only two kilometres by sea from Albania. Can you imagine that – living in Albania during communism, and being so close to democracy? Two kilometres is nothing. Except, of course, it was back then. It might as well have been two thousand kilometres. Border police would shoot anyone who tried to cross, and the water near the Albanian coast was full of mines. Many people still tried to swim to Corfu but a lot died in the process."

Elton told us one story involving a trio of people, two sisters and one brother. Before embarking on their journey, the three bought watermelons, which they hollowed out. These items would be useful in two ways: firstly, as a buoyancy aid, and secondly, as an improvised air canister.

"They set off and managed to swim away from the Albanian coast, avoiding the mines, and without anyone spotting them. But by the time they got to Corfu, only two of them were alive. The brother drowned along the way."

"Well that was a nice story, Elton," I said. "Very uplifting."

Elton smiled. "Yes, I am sorry. But there are many more stories just like that one. People were so desperate to escape Albania."

Nowadays, people cross from the other direction. Excursion companies based on the Greek island, offer day trips to Albania by boat. They are aimed at curious holidaymakers wanting to sample a bit of former communist life. They are very popular.

"Okay," said Elton slowing down. "Please have your passports ready, we are near the border."

5

I only knew two things about Macedonia. One was that it had an extremely good flag. It consisted of a yellow spiky sun splashed across a red background. Simple but highly effective. I thought it was perhaps the greatest flag ever devised. Others thought so too, because, in 2002, the editors of the World Almanac, a US reference book, held a poll to find the top ten flags of the world. Macedonia's came second, only losing out to the flag of Bhutan.

The other thing I knew about Macedonia was to do with its name. Apparently, Greece didn't like the fact it was calling itself *Macedonia*. They claimed, quite rightly, that the term Macedonia referred to a part of northern Greece, and that people living there had been calling themselves Macedonians for over a thousand years. These Greek Macedonians had nothing in common with the people living in the former Yugoslav republic, now masquerading as Macedonia.

The Greeks also took offense at Macedonia claiming that Alexander the Great was Macedonian, when in fact he was *Greek* Macedonian. These issues escalated to the point that the UN had to step in. In the end, they declared that the country should be called *The Former Yugoslav Republic of Macedonia* or FYROM for short.

This didn't really appease the Macedonians, or the Greeks, and it certainly didn't appease Greek Macedonians, but, in 1993, it happened anyway. It was supposed to be a short-term solution, but the name sort of stuck.

The border was another easy affair. Passports were checked, car details were scrutinised, and then we were in. The Former Yugoslav Republic of Macedonia accepted us with grace.

6

With the border disappearing behind us, the four of us settled down for the short journey to Ohrid, the first stop on our Macedonia adventure.

Farmland featured prominently outside, with crop fields interspersed with the occasional sheep, goat and hoe-wielding farmer. I also spied lots of small tractors, but none seemed modern. It was as if we were travelling through 1950s Britain.

A short while later, we arrived at the town of Ohrid, famous for its huge expanse of clear water. As Elton found a parking space, Michael and I looked outside with glee, because Ohrid looked extraordinarily beautiful.

"We will stay here for two hours," Elton informed us. "You can perhaps see the tourist things, while Kaltrina and I get something to eat and visit the shops."

It sounded like a splendid idea and so, waving good-bye to them, Michael and I headed into town.

"Wow," I said as we wandered away from the car. The view in front of us was stunningly gorgeous, with sunlight reflecting off the ripples on the lake. "I had no idea Ohrid would be so nice."

"Nor did I," admitted Michael, already taking a photo.

The old part of town was full of small shops covered in Cyrillic, one displaying a sign that read оптика, *optician*, and another in English that advertised Tattoos and Piercings. Colourful markets, spindly minarets and gushing fountains made up the rest of the old town, and up in the hills were ancient churches, basilicas and red-roofed houses. In fact, Ohrid had an unexpected Mediterranean flavour. We could have been in Greece. No wonder UNESCO had made it a heritage site in 1980. Michael and I headed down through the centre of town until we came to Lake Ohrid, the star attraction of the town.

Stretching for miles, lush green mountains flanked the three million-year-old lake: one of Europe's deepest, we later learned. Boats sloshed about on the calm surface and just in front of the lake was a huge Macedonian flag.

Because Ohrid was such a popular place for tourists, platoons of boat touts called for business along the shoreline. "I give good boat ride," one man said. "Only 300 dinar (£4) for thirty minute trip!" We declined his offer and instead turned away from the serenity of the lake until we came to a cobbled path leading uphill. After twenty minutes of furious hiking, we found ourselves at a small church called Saint John at Kaneo.

7

The small place of worship reminded me of some orthodox churches I'd seen in Armenia. Saint John's was brown, with copper-coloured clay roof tiles, and tiny round windows above a series of arches. It was perched on the cliff edge with a view over the lake.

Because of its prime location, the church featured heavily on postcards of Ohrid, but bizarrely, apart from a man leaning against a fence, we had the monastery to ourselves. After unsuccessfully trying to get inside, we simply stood and admired the view. It was at this point that the man approached us.

He turned out to be a perceptive boat tout, there on the off-chance a couple of tourists would show up, too lazy to walk back into town.

"Church is closed for two hour," he told us. "You can wait, or you can go back to town in my boat. It's up to you."

"Why is it closed?" Michael asked.

"The priest is having lunch."

Neither of us wanted to hang around for two hours, and besides, we had to meet Elton and Kaltrina in about an hour. So, for a small price, the man led us to his boat. To reach the water we had to climb down some almost vertical steps. We jumped aboard and the man soon had us on our way, with clear water swishing around us. High above, on a cliff top ledge was the old fortress walls; it reminded me of Kotor in Montenegro.

8

Michael and I found a quiet cafe in the old town, and ordered lunch. The cafe was at the edge of a square that housed a thousand-year-old maple tree, its thick trunk and sprawling branches offering shade to people passing underneath. Benches surrounded the tree, and a trio of old men were sitting on one, walking sticks by their sides, deep in throaty conversation.

Michael picked up his bottle of Macedonian lager and tried to decipher the Cyrillic name.

"It says Skopsko," I told him, reading the name from my own bottle.

We watched as a family of four walked past. The two children were eating ice-creams.

"Well," I said. "Ohrid gets a thumbs up from me so far. If Skopje is as good as this, then I've got high hopes for Macedonia."

"It won't be. Skopje's supposed to be a concrete jungle. A bit of a shit hole actually, from what I've read."

Our lunch arrived, and was, once again an oil-based affair. Afterwards we headed back to the car to meet Elton and Kaltrina. It was time to travel onwards to the Macedonian capital.

10. Skopje: Macedonia

Interesting fact: Macedonia produces the best quality opium in the world. It is twice as potent as Pakistan's.

The road to Skopje was a vista of vivid mountains, deep gorges, lush vegetation and the occasional farmhouse. Along the way, I saw Elton's girlfriend flicking through the free Skopje guidebook we'd picked up in Ohrid. She stopped at the section describing places to stay.

The list ranked hotels in order, from exclusive to low-budget, and Kaltrina was looking at the offerings in the latter section. Michael and I had already booked our hotel. I knew it was in the low-budget section because I'd already checked.

Suddenly the engine roared as Elton accelerated past a slow-moving truck. Thick black smoke was pouring from the lorry's upright exhaust pipe. After settling back into our side of the road, Elton spotted the page Kaltrina was studying, and then reached over and flipped the page back one. This new list was entitled *dirt cheap*.

Kaltrina scoffed, apparently not liking the look of the cheapest fleapits in Skopje, and quickly flicked back. Elton muttered something in Albanian to her, and once again turned the page back. Resigned, Kaltrina turned to a section entitled *shopping*. No doubt she'd get her revenge there.

A few hours later, Elton announced we were lost. It was late evening and sunset was fast approaching. The highway we'd been driving along had long since disappeared, replaced instead by a minor road frequented by tractors and sluggish lorries.

Elton looked crestfallen. "I do not know what to say. I am not sure how this happened. This road will increase our journey by one and a half hours. I am sorry."

Michael and I were not bothered in the slightest. We had no deadline to meet, and we told Elton this. We drove onwards as the sun began to drop below the distant mountains.

2

Grey, concrete tower blocks, pot-holed roads, and graffiti were everywhere. Bangers clogged the roads and unshaven men stood on street corners looking like they were waiting to rob someone, or else receive a shipment of arms.

The outskirts of Skopje looked grim, especially now that night had fallen. Elton looked agitated too. For the previous ten minutes, he and Kaltrina had been trying to follow a woefully inadequate map. Finally they gave up and pulled into a bus station.

There was a van parked in front of us. Two shady looking men were loading it with beds that they had either stolen or were planning to hide drugs inside. The four of us watched them.

"I will speak to these men," Elton said. He jumped out of the car and walked up to them. A few moments later, all three disappeared around the side of the van, for what I could only presume was a hard beating. Evidently, Kaltrina thought the same thing too because she looked flustered and opened her door. "Stay here," she said as she climbed out. She followed after them.

I looked at Michael. It was dark outside and we wondered what to do. Should we wait in the car, as we'd been told, or climb out to see what was going on?

"I'm not sure," admitted Michael, but just then our choices were made redundant, because Elton and Kaltrina reappeared, safe and sound. The bed packers did too. Everyone was smiling and shaking hands.

 "These men will show us where the hotel is," said Elton as he climbed into the driver's seat. "They said we can follow their van."

I shook my head in wonderment. Some complete strangers had become our saviours in Skopje. Fifteen minutes later we were parked outside our small hotel. The men drove away, waving as they rounded a corner.

We had arrived in the Macedonian capital.

3

After some quick discussion, Elton and Kaltrina decided to stay in the same hotel as us, clearly not relishing the prospect of getting lost again. Agreeing to meet in the hotel bar after depositing our things, Michael and I went up to our room, where I had my first encounter with a hotel toilet turd.

It was floating there, mocking me, bobbing up and down, resolutely refusing to be flushed away. Michael eventually dispatched the beast with some serious flushing and poking, and came out sweating, but triumphant.

To celebrate, we had a Skopsko with Elton and Kaltrina. As we chatted, I remembered a book I'd read by Tony Hawks entitled *One Hit Wonderland*. In it, he'd taken a bet whereby he had to score a hit single somewhere in Europe. One of the places Hawks visited was Albania.

Well-known British comedian Norman Wisdom had joined him on his trip. In the book, Hawks described Norman Wisdom as being a hero to the people of Albania, and hoped that a song featuring the great man would be a hit. I wanted to test Tony Hawks' theory out on Elton and Kaltrina.

"Have either of you heard of a man called Norman Wisdom?" I asked.

Both visibly cheered at the mention of the comedian's name. They smiled and began speaking in quick Albanian, no doubt recounting some of Mr Wisdom's finer moments. Elton spoke first. "He is known as Mr Pitkin in my country, because of a character he played in a movie. He is like a folk hero to the Albanian people. During the communist era, Pitkin was only one of three Western comedians allowed on TV. The other two were Laurel and Hardy. Enver Hoxha was a big fan. It was sad when he died."

How strange, I thought: a couple of twenty-something Albanians with such fond memories of an old British comedian. I wondered how many young people from England had even *heard* of Norman Wisdom. After saying goodbye to Elton and Kaltrina, Michael and I wandered off to see what Skopje had to offer. Our new Albanian friends needed an early night because they were heading back to Tirana first thing in the morning.

4

Street lighting was not a priority concern in downtown Skopje, because dark alleyways led us between tower blocks bathed in shadows. We passed the *Sexy Shop*, its gaudy red neon lettering advertising private video booths. Another store sold only sellotape, the first shop of its kind I'd seen anywhere in the world. Reels of it hung behind the window, or sat coiled upon shelves.

"Have your testicles started swelling up yet?" I asked Michael, causing him to almost choke on his Skopsko. We were sat in a city centre restaurant, the one area of the capital that seemed well lit. "It's just that Macedonia is having its biggest mumps outbreak of the last 25 years, and that's one of the symptoms."

After regaining his composure, Michael assured me that his tackle was normal-sized, and so we got down to business and ordered some food.

Dal Met Fu Restaurant turned out to be a good choice. Firstly, the food was decent and cheap. Secondly, the waitresses were all gorgeous and wore the shortest skirts possible (a fact proudly illustrated in their advertising leaflet), but the third and best reason was found in the toilets.

"Wait till you see the sinks," Michael told me, after returning from a visit. With my interest piqued, I headed off, wondering what he'd found. The sinks were standard issue apart from one key feature – they had no taps or sensors! Instead, they utilised a couple of foot pedals, red for hot, blue for cold, and I pressed both with childish glee until a man arrived. He stared at me with suspicion. I dried my hands and left.

"Come on," I said to Michael a few minutes later, "Let's find a bar."

After a few drinks in some centrally located bars, we headed through the darkened streets of Skopje back towards the hotel.

5

The next morning was sunny again. Michael and I had been lucky with the weather on our trip around the Balkans. There had only been one real downpour, and that was on the way from Dubrovnik to Kotor.

Michael had a cap on his head, a camera in his pocket and a map in his brain. Every now and again he would stop walking and rotate his head, as if searching for a good satellite signal. Sometimes I thought he was half robot.

We were heading to Skopje's old railway station, now a museum. Earlier, over breakfast (a strange conglomeration of a boiled egg, a triangular piece of foil-wrapped cheese and a small chocolate biscuit called *pop kek*), Michael had insisted that we visit it, saying we hadn't been in a museum for days.

Even doused in sunlight, no one would describe the southern part of Skopje as beautiful. It was full of concrete and tower blocks. As we crossed a busy road, I was also struck by the sheer number of dilapidated cars. Ancient Yugos, Ladas and Skodas were all over the city, or at least along the route we were walking. If ever there was a city where old communist cars could go to die, then Skopje was it. Many were abandoned on paths and pavements, often with plants and weeds growing over them, sometimes with vegetation inside their interiors.

"The museum is just around this street," said Michael, striding forwards. I trudged after him, to what would be the first of three museums I'd visit that day.

6

According to the *Macedonian Weekly News*, 330 small tremors had occurred near the Macedonian border only a few days prior to our arrival. But these were nothing compared to the earthquake that struck Skopje in 1963.

The earthquake started at 5.17am, and, despite lasting only a few seconds, killed over a thousand people, and left 200,000 homeless. The old railway station was one of the buildings partially destroyed, and its clock face was frozen at the exact time the earthquake had stopped it.

Michael and I stared up at the hands. They did indeed show the time of the earthquake, just a little nudge over quarter past five. The clock was located above the entrance to the museum, a section of the building that looked structurally sound. The bit adjoining it, however, looked in bad shape, with broken arches and crumbling brickwork.

"Right," I said wearily. "Let's get this over with."

The museum was dull, featuring a collection of ancient pots and other such artefacts. The only real item of interest was a large black and white photograph of what Skopje had looked like before the earthquake. It showed the famous stone bridge and a set of grand-looking buildings in a square beyond. But even with the photo, after just seven minutes, I was back outside. Michael took a further three minutes.

"Hmm," he said when he joined me. He was taking a photo of the damaged section next to the entrance. "It wasn't as good as I hoped. The building itself is much more interesting than the contents. Let's head for the centre. I want to see a memorial to Mother Teresa."

7

Mother Teresa was born in Skopje, and to commemorate this great fact, a large statue of her stood near a small rectangular building in the centre of the city. The Memorial House to Mother Teresa seemed a mishmash of styles to me. Old stone arches, jutting modern verandas, and blue-glassed blocks competed for attention. It looked like three or four different architects had assembled a job lot of ideas into one. I thought it looked ugly.

Michael disagreed. He loved the thing, and, while I sat on a nearby wall, he circled the odd building, taking photos from every angle. "Whoever designed it," he told me a few minutes later, "got it exactly right. Let's go in."

Reluctantly, I followed him towards my second museum of the day.

The main part of the museum showed the living conditions Mother Teresa *might* have lived in as a little girl. There was a bed, a table and chairs, and some old wardrobes to look at. A party of ten-year-old schoolchildren wearing small knapsacks were already there, crowding around a guide who was describing some photos. I bypassed the gaggle, and, after pausing to look at some letters written by the actual nun, I moved upstairs. There I found a small chapel, but the people praying put me off lingering for too long. I left the museum, and sat back down on the wall to wait for Michael.

"What is your problem with museums?" he asked, twenty minutes later.

I looked at him blankly.

"Because I'm starting to think you're a cultural heathen. I mean, you visit all these different countries, and you see all these wonderful things, but when it actually comes to learning a little bit about them, you run a mile. I don't think I've ever been in a museum that you've enjoyed."

"Not true," I interjected. "I enjoyed the Tunnel Museum in Sarajevo, and the one we visited in Bratislava. And I didn't mind the one in Kiev about Chernobyl."

"Yes, but they were not the usual kind of museums, were they? They were specialist museums, more like interactive displays. And that one in Bratislava was just full of torture equipment."

I nodded. "Yeah, and it had no pots in it."

Michael could see that he wasn't going to sway my opinion of museums, and so suggested we visit the old bridge instead.

I agreed.

8

The Ottomans constructed Turkish baths, mosques, a large fortress and a mighty bridge that spanned the turbulent River Vardar. The famous Stone Bridge, a long arched crossing that reminded me of the Latin Bridge in Sarajevo, was one of the major tourist attractions of Skopje. Not that there were many tourists.

The Turks had built the bridge so well that it had managed to withstand fires, floods, and the deadly ravages of the 1963 earthquake. Even some Nazi explosives planted under the bridge during World War Two had not managed to destroy it. Allied troops had deactivated them during the liberation of Skopje.

As well as being a crossing point, the Turks had used the bridge to carry out public executions. Usually they hanged people from the side, but they also carried out a few impalements on its gentle arch. The bridge had possessed a set of thin pillars, perfect for squeezing a criminal's head onto.

Today, the Stone Bridge is a major pedestrian link between the more modern (and concrete heavy) south of the river, and the old Turkish north. To reach it, we had to pass through Macedonia Square, an area almost destroyed by the earthquake. One building that escaped the destruction was the Ristik Palace, a six-storey 1920s structure, named after its then owner. Nowadays, the palace contains shops and has a huge Skopsko advertising boarding on the top.

Major construction work was going on across the other side of the river. Cranes littered the ground, but the buildings they were servicing looked impressive, even in their unfinished state. However, the main draw of Macedonia Square was undoubtedly the massive statue in the middle.

Standing on a mammoth pedestal (which doubled up as a fountain) was a gigantic bronze man sitting on top of a metal horse. The horse was rearing up, making the man seem even more warrior-like, especially with his colossal sword thrust into the air. The Macedonian authorities had been careful not to say who the man was, simply calling him Warrior on a Horse. But everyone knew he was Alexander the Great.

After admiring the statue, we headed towards the bridge.

9

The River Vardar was a torrent of dark grey. Spray from eddies and undercurrents almost reached the bridge. As far as we could tell, there were no boats plying the waterway, and the only people we could see were a trio of fishermen, their rods dangling into the rapids.

The northern side of Skopje reminded me a little of Sarajevo. It had spindly minarets, and stalls selling brightly coloured carpets and spices, all adding a touch of exoticness to the city. On our right was an old Turkish bathhouse, its domes now covering an art gallery. Closer still, at street level, the smell of kebabs filled the air. I decided I quite liked Skopje.

A few minutes later, we found ourselves inside a large bazaar, which was a ramshackle collection of stalls selling the usual array of goods. It was next to a busy road, where people had parked their cars wherever they liked. Nearby, a few men sat at small wooden tables, selling packets of cigarettes to passers-by.

Michael and I walked past them, and waited for a gap in the traffic. We wanted to get to a clock tower we had seen. Clock towers had become our *thing* on the Balkan Odyssey.

10

Like many former Ottoman towns, Skopje had quite a few clock towers. Historically, whenever the call to prayer had sounded from their lofty positions, trading in the bazaars had to cease. This was to stop one merchant from taking advantage of another. The tall tower Michael and I were traipsing towards dated from the 16th century.

We passed a secondary school. It was in a state of disrepair, its students hanging around or leaving by the entrance. I looked at my watch and realised it was lunchtime. Michael and I carried on walking along a looping road.

"I reckon we cut through this alley," said Michael, pointing between two broken-down buildings. An abandoned white Yugo had been left at the side of the road. The scene looked like one from a cold war film. From somewhere, we could hear the sound of teenagers laughing.

We headed down the alley, hoping it would lead us to the clock tower, because, to me, we seemed to be in the midst of a residential area. And not a nice one. We passed a series of brick walls and decrepit outbuildings, most of which had lines of washing suspended between them. Then we arrived at a wire fence. It surrounded an open area of wasteland. The clock tower was in the middle.

"At least we're here," said Michael, already searching for a gap in the fence. I stared through the wire at the tower and adjoining mosque. Michael shouted for my attention. He had found a gap.

The whole place was deserted, covered in undergrowth. No one was around. We wondered what to do. "Do you reckon it's even open?" Michael asked me.

"I'm not sure."

We were still some distance away from the tower but close enough to see just how high it was. It was much taller than the other towers we'd climbed. If it had been in silhouette, it could have formed the cover of a Stephen King novel.

We walked to the base of the tower until we arrived at a large wooden door. It looked ancient, like something from a vampire film. We pulled the large handle but were not surprised to find it locked. Just then a man appeared from a house we had not even noticed before. He looked at us suspiciously.

I smiled, and gestured that we wanted to climb the tower. The man stared at us for a few moments, and then walked back into his little house. Maybe he was going to ring the police. Michael and I were just about to turn tail when another man appeared from the same building, this one older. He was sporting a blue shirt and grey moustache. "Wait!" the new man yelled. He hurried towards us.

11

"Tower?" he said, smiling. "You want to go up?"

Michael and I nodded, and so the man produced a large metal key from his pocket, the sort seen in medieval films. He pressed it into the lock, and with a grind from the inner workings, the door opened.

"I am Imam from mosque," the man said, stepping into the darkness. "I also caretaker of clock tower. Come."

As soon as we stepped into the interior, I began to regret our decision to visit the tower. There was nothing inside, apart from a rickety wooden staircase, which led upwards into the gloom. Before I could say anything however, the Imam was climbing the first few steps, pausing only to tell us to watch our heads. Michael followed him, and then so did I.

"Oh my God," I whispered to Michael, trying to keep my voice down so the Imam wouldn't hear. "This is not a good idea at all."

Michael didn't answer me. He simply followed the Imam upwards.

Beneath my feet, the wood was creaking, and the gaps in some of the steps looked wide enough to fit my arm. I was feeling mightily uncomfortable, and the more I thought about it, the worse I felt.

My heart was pounding, and my hands were sweating. Why was I putting myself through this, I wondered? And what if the stairs were not strong enough to hold our combined weight? When was the last time anyone had climbed them? The groans they made with every step suggested imminent collapse. I gripped the stone walls of the tower, wishing I was sitting in a bar somewhere.

We reached the top and found ourselves in a small wooden compartment. Above our heads was a large bell, and around the edge were some small windows. They allowed slivers of light to enter.

I glanced at the bell, and then at the Imam and Michael. Both seemed happy to be in the bell room. I looked downwards, wondering how I'd managed to climb up. Even the wooden flooring we were standing on didn't seem safe. I imagined a split forming, then turning into a thick fissure, and, with a sickening crack, we'd be falling downwards, tumbling through the blackness, screaming all the way.

"Okay," said the Imam. "Follow me please. Now we go outside!"

12

The Imam unbolted a tiny door and squeezed himself through. Michael looked undaunted by the prospect of stepping outside, but I was almost palpitating with fear. After Michael disappeared through the gap, I reluctantly followed them.

If climbing the tower had caused a growing feeling of dread, then stepping onto the tiny platform was terrifying. I could hardly breathe, and my head was starting to spin. As Michael later pointed out, the tiny metal railings at the edge would not have halted our descent had we slipped, they would've merely added to the head trauma. The safety railings barely reached my waist, and I began to feel truly afraid.

"There are thirty three mosques in Skopje," said the Imam, blithely unaware of the terror he'd unleashed. He pointed one out in the distance, and began describing it. I tried to concentrate on what he was saying, but all I could imagine was falling to my doom. My back was pressed so hard against the wall of the tower that it hurt. I'd spread my hands out too, but they were offering precious little comfort. I wondered for one brief moment whether I should grab Michael's hand.

The Imam looked at us. "And there are over five hundred mosques in the whole of Macedonia," he said, seemingly incapable of feeling any fear. "And down there is the bazaar. Look: you can see it."

I lowered my gaze by a few degrees but immediately raised it. At the same time, I increased my deathgrip on the wall. There was no way I was going to look down, that was for sure. The sight of Skopje's red roofs and grey concrete blocks was enough for me. Michael was braver, actually taking a photo. Then the Imam began moving around the edge of the tower. "Come," he said.

Michael followed him, but I decided to stay put. I was going to try to back myself through the door. With my hands, I tried to feel my way in, but only succeeded in almost tripping on the upturned step. My stomach lurched as a surge of panic rose through me. If I'd have fallen, I could have toppled down the staircase.

"Come on," shouted Michael as he disappeared around the curve of the tower. I didn't answer him. Instead, I considered dropping to my hands and knees, but the thought of such drastic movement made me recoil. Besides, the walkway probably wasn't wide enough for me to crouch onto. My legs were shaking and I felt like throwing up. I waited for Michael and the Imam to make a complete circuit. They did so a few minutes later, and both helped me back inside.

Twenty minutes later, Michael and I found a bar overlooked by another statue of Skanderbeg, the hero of Albania we'd seen a few days previously. My hands were still trembling.

"I know it was a bit on the dangerous side," said Michael. "But I really enjoyed that tower."

I took a large slug of my beer, feeling my pulse slowly returning to *panic stations* as opposed to *terror alert*. The views had been impressive, the Imam friendly, and the adrenalin rush out of this world, but I never wanted to step foot into such a precarious position again.

13

Kapan Han was just around the corner from the bar. Built in the 15th century by an Ottoman general, it had once been a medieval inn. The pretty courtyard was where the animals of passing merchants were kept, while the men slept in the rooms above. It was similar to an inn we had visited in Sarajevo. Nowadays, the courtyard was free of animals, except for a curious cat who stared as we took our seats in the courtyard cafe.

The cafe served traditional Macedonian food, and so I ordered *country meats in sauce*, while Michael opted for *meat covered in vine leaves*. Both were delicious and reasonably priced, as everything in Skopje was. And better still, my meal came devoid of oil.

"I know you'll probably say no..." said Michael between mouthfuls. "And I know you've already been in two today..."

"Not another museum?"

Michael put his fork down. "This one is called the National Museum of Macedonia, and it's actually three museums in one: the archaeological, the historical and the ethno-"

"Three museums in one? You've got to be joking? Are they full of pots and spears, and old bits of cloth?"

"Probably. But it's the last museum I'll ask you to go in. And I'll buy you a couple of Skopskos tonight. Plus...there's a pot you might even like..."

I scoffed. "Why?"

"You'll see."

14

The National Museum of Macedonia was not far from the old bazaar, but, as I'd feared, it was massive. And as usual, as soon as we stepped inside, Michael and I separated: him to read and study every exhibit, me to rush around ancient coins, traditional costumes and rooms full of pots.

I thought about what Michael had said to me earlier. He'd accused me of being a heathen, not erudite enough to appreciate the historical artefacts found in museums. I paused at a large glass cabinet holding a collection of bowls. I stared at them, searching for inspiration but found nothing. Maybe he was right. To me, they were just old bowls. The next cabinet had more of the same. I moved on.

Upstairs was slightly better. It was a large and darkened room full of religious icons. Some of them dated back to the 11th century. The gold leaf and vibrant reds made the whole room look magical. I lingered in the icon room long enough for Michael to catch me up.

"Did you see the pot?" he whispered.

"Which one? I saw hundreds of pots."

"You didn't see it then."

I looked at Michael. "Which pot are you talking about?"

"The one I said you'd like. Go back downstairs and find it. You'll know when you see it. It's in a cabinet all by itself."

I left Michael with the icons, retracing my steps, walking around cabinets filled with bowls, jugs and clay cups. My eyes scanned the exhibits but saw nothing remotely interesting. I was just about to give up when I spotted it. My eyes widened in surprise. Michael was right – it was a strange item. I rushed up to the cabinet to study it further.

It was a jug shaped like an erect penis, the spout jutting upwards at an unmistakable angle. The caption told me it was a fertility symbol. I snapped a quick photo, shaking my head that someone had actually fashioned the thing. It looked like the work of an adolescent clay maker. I joined Michael in the icon room again.

"Good, isn't it?" he sniggered.

Half an hour later, we left the museum and headed uphill.

15

Skopje, I was surprised to learn, actually had an old fort perched on a hill. It was just north of the city centre, and was known as Kale Fortress.

The fortress walls offered a good view of the city. "What's that horrible thing?" I asked, pointing at a hideous monstrosity masquerading as a building. It had strange protruding arms of concrete, with a weird dome in the middle. If it was painted silver, it might resemble someone's idea of a 1930s spaceship.

"That'll be the post office," answered Michael.

We headed down from the fortress towards it. Up close, it looked even worse. It no longer reminded me of a concrete spaceship; instead it resembled a maximum-security prison. I wondered why anyone would want to build such a thing. It was possibly the ugliest building I'd ever seen. We carried on past it until we came to a row of brightly coloured Macedonian flags. They were in front of a grand-looking building. As Michael knelt to take a photo, a guard appeared.

"No photo!" he shouted, waving his arms in a cross. "Government building! Leave now!"

Suitably chastised, Michael put his camera away and we headed back to the centre of the city.

16

One hour later, a hellish storm erupted. Thunder and lightning blasted the sky, sending rain down in torrents. Rivers formed in roads, and every pothole became a pool of dark water. But this didn't concern us, because we were sitting in a bar enjoying a couple of Skopskos, all paid for by Michael. For almost an hour, the storm raged, before finally weakening.

"Right," I said. "Back to the hotel to pack. We're almost at the end of the Odyssey. Only Kosovo left."

Michael stopped flicking through the photos he'd taken on his camera and looked up. "How many countries have we been to so far?"

"Seven," I said. "Serbia, Bosnia, Slovenia, Croatia, Montenegro, Albania and now Macedonia."

Michael nodded. "Not bad going, really."

"No," I agreed. "Not bad at all."

11. Pristina, Kosovo

Interesting fact: The word, Kosovo, translates as Land of Blackbirds.

The next morning, the ravages of the storm were gone, leaving only a fine mist clinging to the hills. After a quick breakfast, Michael and I were ready to rock. We caught a cheap taxi to Skopje Bus Station, and, after Michael had bought some tickets, we waited for our onwards transport.

The bus station was another concrete affair, located beneath a busy underpass. Cars and lorries shook the roof as they passed overhead. A few other people were already waiting for the Pristina-bound bus, including a middle-aged man in a striped T-shirt, a well-dressed, grey-haired lady holding a brief case, and a man carrying a car radiator as hand luggage.

When the big white bus arrived, we all trooped aboard and sat down.

2

Kosovo had hit the headlines in the 1990s for all the wrong reasons. Ethnic cleansing, NATO air strikes, Albanian refugees and accusations of war crimes on both sides meant Kosovo became synonymous with everything that was wrong in the Balkans.

After the worst of the fighting had died down, and Serbian troops pulled out, the UN installed peacekeepers. They were needed to provide neutrality between ethnic Albanians (the majority of Kosovo's population) and ethnic Serbs. Bit by bit, Kosovo stabilised.

In 2008, after a prolonged period of relative peace, Kosovo declared itself independent from Serbia. A few countries recognised its independence, including the UK, USA and Australia, but Serbia didn't, and nor did Russia and China. And, as our bus travelled towards the border, the issue remained unresolved.

3

According to the British Foreign Office website, Kosovo still had plenty of unexploded landmines; it therefore advised against travelling off the beaten track. The website also told us to keep alert at all times, and to avoid any demonstrations. Kosovo would be the edgiest place Michael and I had visited since crossing into Transnistria the previous year. Transnistria was a communist breakaway republic: officially part of Moldova; unofficially, a de facto Soviet-style republic. We'd enjoyed it immensely.

The bus journey from Skopje to the border was uneventful, stopping every now and again to pick up passengers. At the Macedonian border, the bus came to a standstill so we could hand our passports to a woman who wandered down the aisles. She diligently checked our faces against the photos inside. That done, we drove through no-man's land until we came to the Kosovo border.

Military 4x4s sat parked near the customs building, and armed men stood about smoking cigarettes. They looked as hard as nails. Eventually, our passports came back pasted with Kosovo stamps. It was official; we were going to be allowed entry.

With a lurch, the bus trundled into the Republic of Kosovo, and then came to a shuddering standstill as the engine conked out. The border guards seemed to think this was amusing, but we ended up having the last laugh, because when the bus finally got going, it left a black belch of cancerous smoke in its wake.

Just past the border was an ugly town, mainly made up of cement factories and their associated quarries. Trucks filled with building materials chugged between them. Then, as the factories made way for farmland, Michael and I stared at the hills in the distance. Two military helicopters were flying above them. We were actually in a country with UN peacekeepers!

4

The large truck in front of us was hindering our progress. We were travelling along a single lane highway, and our bus did not possess the oomph to overtake the slower lorry. With a couple of hours still to go, I settled back, and closed my eyes. Michael had already contented himself with a paperback.

Michael had been the perfect travelling companion, I realised. He liked visiting the same places as me, he liked the odd tipple, and he was certainly not fazed by anything out of the ordinary. And he had a head like a GPS. Drop him in any city in the world, and within minutes, he'd have the lay of the land etched in his brain. His only downfalls were his insistence on visiting museums and his pathological desire to take a photo of everything he saw.

"Michael?" I said. "What are my failings as a travel companion?"

Michael folded over the corner of the page, and closed his book. He gazed at the scenery outside for a moment. It was more countryside. Eventually he looked at me and said, "I'm not sure."

"Well have a think. And don't say anything about museums. We've already covered that."

While Michael thought about my failings, I looked at the woman opposite. Her briefcase was on the empty seat next to her, and she was reading a book. She sensed me staring and looked up. She smiled and I smiled back.

"I know," announced Michael. "You always moan about food."

"Food?"

"Yeah. I've lost count of the meals we've had when you've moaned about food. *Ooh, this is too oily! Ooh, this has too many onions in it! Ooh, I can't eat this, it's got butter on the bread! Ooh, this isn't what I expected!*"

"Really? I moan about food a lot?"

"All the time. Especially on planes. Every meal you get, you moan about."

"Okay. Anything else that annoys you?" I would be keeping track of my food moaning from now on.

Michael laughed. "I didn't say that you complaining about food annoys me; it's just something I've noticed you doing. As for anything else...I don't know...oh hang on...I know – you snore!"

I nodded, pleased that he'd only been able to think of two things. "So I moan about food and I snore. I don't think that's too bad. We've spent nearly three weeks together and they're the only things you can think of? I'm happy with that."

"What about me?" asked Michael, now interested in the conversation. "What are my weaknesses?"

"Where to begin," I said heavily. "You annoy me with your eating. It's the way you slurp stuff down – it makes me want to throw up. I don't like your feet as well, they're too large for your body. And I don't like your big, bald head because it offends me. Shall I carry on?"

Michael picked up his book.

"Actually, Michael, not much about you annoys me."

He nodded, and began to read.

5

Apart from farms and rolling hills, Kosovo appeared to be a land of scrapyards. They were everywhere, some even catering purely for mangled trucks.

We were still behind the lorry, but, as our bus reached the top of a hill, we hit a stretch of highway long enough for our driver to attempt an insane overtaking manoeuvre.

Hitting full steam, our bus gained momentum. When we were just behind the truck, our driver swung into the other side of the road. Inch by inch we crept forward, until the front of both vehicles were parallel. I considered waving at the lorry driver, but my attention was drawn to the front. A juggernaut was hurtling towards us from the opposite direction.

I could already imagine the headlines our wives would read. *Killed in Kosovo: Hapless Brits involved in deadly bus carnage.* But, thankfully, disaster was averted when both lorry drivers realised what was going to happen, and braked heavily. It allowed our bus a precious second to slip into the gap.

Dotted around villages, or sometimes in the middle of nowhere, a few mosques stood. Many of them had silver domes that glinted in the sun. But quite a lot of them didn't have minarets. I pointed this out to Michael. The woman with the briefcase opposite must have overheard me, because she addressed us in an American accent.

"The reason for the lack of minarets," she said, "is that, during the Kosovo War, Serb troops used them as target practice."

The lady turned out to be a UN economist working in Pristina. She told us that she travelled between Kosovo and Skopje fairly regularly. She was a little surprised to find out Michael and I were tourists.

"What's Pristina like?" Michael asked.

"Dusty," she answered. "And the traffic is bad, but it does have its nice areas. Just watch out for the potholes, and missing manhole covers. Where you staying?"

"The Grand Hotel," I said.

The lady nodded. "It's a nice hotel in a good location. Everything is within walking distance, so you boys won't need a cab."

"That's good. But is there anything we should be aware of?" I asked. "I mean, things we need to be careful about?"

"Can you speak Serbian?"

Both of us shook our heads.

"Then that's okay. Because that could get you into trouble. What you have to understand is that Pristina is almost all ethnic

Albanians. If people hear you speaking Serbian they might take offence. Tensions are high between the Albanians and Serbs. I'll tell you a little story. Back in 1999, a Bulgarian UN worker was sent to Pristina. He was fluent is six languages, and on his first day in Kosovo he was walking down Mother Teresa Street – that's the street where your hotel is – when some young Albanian men asked him the time. But they didn't ask the question in Albanian, they asked it in Serb-Croat, because they thought he might be a Serb due to his dark skin complexion. And even though this guy was fluent in Albanian, he answered in Serb-Croat. So these young Albanians now think he's definitely a Serb. They surround him and start attacking him. Others join in and the poor guy is dragged away somewhere. He was found dead the next day with a bullet in his head."

"Jesus," I said. "That's terrible."

"Yeah. But that was over ten years ago. Things have calmed down since then. You boys will be safe."

Just then there was an almighty grinding noise, and the bus came to a dramatic halt.

"Not again," said the woman, sighing. "This is all I need."

6

We were thirty kilometres from Pristina, and the driver had parked the bus on the side of the road. He and the conductor quickly climbed out, closely followed by the man who had brought the car radiator, though he left the item on his seat. Maybe it was a spare part for the bus, I hoped. After disappearing from sight for a few moments, the driver reappeared with a handful of tools.

"This happens to me all the time," said the American lady. "You would think I'd be used to it by now, but I'm not."

A few passengers got off to have cigarettes, and I decided to buy a drink from a nearby shop. Luckily, we had broken down near a petrol station. When I climbed out, I saw that a large compartment of the bus was open, and some random bits of engine were lying on the ground.

A fellow passenger noticed me looking. "This bus is broken down," he said, stating the obvious. "It will not be repaired for long time. But driver says other bus will come soon."

I thanked him and went into the shop.

Twenty minutes later, a second bus did indeed pull up, and we all swapped vehicles, even the man with the radiator. He removed it from the stricken bus and transported it to the new one. Soon we were on our way again.

We began a gentle descent into the outskirts of Pristina. The city was in the grip of mass building work, giving it the look of a dirty, overgrown building site. Divisions of JCBs were parked all over the place, and shops selling building materials were doing a roaring trade. Men were busy along roadsides, digging holes in the ground.

Soon we arrived in central Pristina, and, as we pulled into the bus station, we could see some new-looking buildings. There must have been a job lot of shiny, blue glass going spare, because most of the buildings were covered in it.

The American woman told us not to pay more than three euros for a taxi to the hotel. She was not going into the city centre, she said, otherwise we could have shared a taxi. The man with the car radiator ignored the taxis and carried his item off down the road.

Michael and I said goodbye to the American woman, and jumped in a taxi. Soon we were speeding past road works towards the centre.

Pristina had a heavy police presence. From the window of the taxi, we could see that they were patrolling the streets in vans or 4x4s. EU peacekeepers were in attendance too: German, Italian and Greek troops were only some of the soldiers we saw. Another military helicopter flew overhead as we checked into the Pristina Grand Hotel.

7

Beautiful and beguiling were not words to describe Pristina. Dusty, chaotic, and ugly would perhaps be more fitting. The pavements were cracked, the roads were potholed, the concrete buildings utterly charmless, and there were plenty of beggars about, too. Some were small children, curled on the ground, wailing loudly to attract maximum attention.

We stopped in one of the bars that lined Mother Teresa Boulevard, a long pedestrianised walkway named after the famous nun. A statue of her was close by. We ordered a couple of bottles of Birra Peja. Men wearing suits wandered by, as did young women in skin-tight jeans. The beer, I noticed, began its life in 1971, making it as old as me.

After posing by another statue of Albanian hero Skanderbeg, we passed a tall skyscraper that served as a Kosovo government building, and then came to a white metal fence lined with A4 photos. Known as the Photos of the Missing, the pictures were of people not seen since 1999, the year of the Kosovo War. One showed a teenager called Jahe Kamer Rukolli, who was born in 1981. The young face looked full of hope. He went missing aged 18.

Hundreds of men and women had gone missing during the Kosovo conflict, mainly due to Serb troops expelling them from their villages. Nobody knew what had happened to them. The sad fact of the matter was, that even by 2013, Kosovo was still discovering possible mass grave sites. And Serbia too was waiting to find out the fate of some of its people. In August 2012, Amnesty International claimed that, in total, 14,000 people were still unaccounted for due to the Balkan Wars. Their families simply wanted closure.

8

The people on the streets of Kosovo were going about their business as they might in any other city. The presence of armoured vehicles at certain intersections did not hinder them as they moved about, and, as Michael and I wandered away from the Photos of the Missing, we could not detect one element of menace. Everyone seemed friendly, laid back even.

The old town of Pristina was slightly prettier than the new, but only just. It was still clogged with vehicles, either trying to push their way through the traffic, or else attempting to park in random places. Buildings were mostly dull-coloured, often with cracked brickwork and missing roof tiles. Pristina was not in a rush to wow tourists with its beauty.

In front of us was the beige Carshi Mosque, Pristina's oldest building. It dated from the 15th century. Back in its prime, its single minaret had towered over a busy bazaar, but the market was long gone, replaced by roads, and a hideous thing called the Monument of Brotherhood Unity. It looked like an upside down concrete dart.

Constructed when Kosovo had still been part of Yugoslavia, the monument was actually three separate towers joined at the top to symbolise the unity of the three main ethnic groups: the Albanians, Serbs and Montenegrins. Clearly the sentiment behind the tower had failed on many levels, because a shroud of barbed wire surrounded the base, stopping locals from vandalising it.

Although the historical bazaar was no longer there, a ramshackle market did exist. It was a hotbed of fruit, vegetables, cigarette stalls and low-lying telephone wires. Packets of cigarettes were stacked like walls around male vendors sitting under large parasols.

"Well, what do you think of Pristina?" I asked Michael as we wandered around the stalls. Children who should have been in school were running around, chasing one another. Stout ladies with dyed hair regarded them with annoyance. Plenty of men were wandering around with plastic bags, often with mobile phones pressed against their ears. I wondered whether they had jobs.

"It's not that great, to be honest. But better than I expected. Give it time though..."

We left the market to find Bill Clinton.

9

The USA had been one of the first countries to recognise Kosovo's independence, and, to show their gratitude, the Pristina authorities decided to build a statue (and name a whole street) after the then president, Bill Clinton.

His boulevard was a long stretch of road lined with shops and ugly apartment blocks. Cars and Mercedes taxis chugged their way along, passing people waiting at bus stops. After a long walk Michael and I arrived at the 11-foot statue of Clinton, one arm outstretched – almost Lenin-like – the other arm clutching documents etched with the date that NATO began airstrikes against Yugoslavia: 24th March 1999. Above the statue, on a giant billboard was the massive face of Bill Clinton gazing out across Pristina. Below him was an advertisement for a brand of tea.

The Kosovo War lasted between February 1988 and June 1999. Its origins lay in the historical tension between the Serbian and Albanian communities of Kosovo. Josip Tito had managed to keep a lid on this tension, mainly by repressing all forms of nationalism.

In the 1980s, as Michael had already explained to me, the people of Kosovo began to demand greater autonomy. They wanted the same rights as the other six republics of Yugoslavia, as opposed to simply being part of Serbia. Belgrade told them to shut up and stop whingeing. Demonstrations broke out, and riot police were sent in. Some protesters were killed and hundreds more were imprisoned. The demonstrations died down, but tensions between Serbs and Albanians escalated.

Albanian citizens started attacking Serb citizens. Christian places of worship were damaged, all of which resulted in thousands of Serbs uprooting and moving out of the Kosovo region.

When Yugoslavia started to disintegrate, Kosovo seized its chance, but Belgrade came down hard, sacking 80,000 Albanians from state jobs in Kosovo, and replacing them all with Serbs. TV broadcasts in Albanian were stopped, and 800 Albanian lecturers from the University of Pristina were told to pack up and leave. The ethnic Albanian majority living in Kosovo felt as if they were being treated as second-class citizens.

In 1996, an ethnic Albanian organisation called the Kosovo Liberation Army (KLA) started attacking Serbian troops. At first the Serbs portrayed the KLA as terrorists (a description backed by the USA), but, when KLA attacks escalated, the Serbs struck back, killing 16 Albanian fighters. And so it spiralled. Serb troops would enter villages and expel any Albanians they found. KLA fighters would try to stop them. Hundreds of thousands of Albanian refugees were the result.

Ceasefires came and went. In the village of Racak, KLA operatives killed four Serbian policemen. In response, Serb forces surrounded, and then stormed, the village. After finding 25 men hiding in a building, Serb troops took them to a nearby hill. The men were all shot dead.

Albanians claimed that the men were innocents, mainly farmers and labourers, with no ties to the KLA. They also claimed that the black-clad Serb troops had tortured and mutilated the men before shooting them. The Serbs disagreed, saying the deaths had resulted after a lengthy fire-fight. Whatever the reason, the Racak Massacre, as it became known, became a turning point in the conflict. NATO now became directly involved.

NATO airstrikes began in March 1999, targeting Serb air defences and military posts in and around Kosovo. But it didn't stop the fighting on the ground. Ethnic cleansing was still going on.

NATO upped the ante and began airstrikes on Belgrade itself. Finally, the Serbs backed down, and allowed peacekeeping troops to occupy Kosovo. Almost immediately, half a million Albanian refugees returned home, and 164,000 Serbs left. No wonder tensions remained high in Kosovo. No wonder Bill Clinton had a statue.

10

In most other cities, the Palace of Youth and Sport would not even warrant a mention, but, with sights so few and far between, we headed for this most prime of Pristina's landmarks.

Built in 1977, it was communist architecture at its best. The abnormality featured concrete blocks sticking out at all sorts of strange angles, and was home to a shopping centre, a cinema and a sports hall.

"And that man there," Michael told me, gesturing to a huge billboard of a bearded gentleman holding a gun, "is Adem Jashari. He was a Kosovo Liberation Army commander killed by the Serbian Police. He's a local hero here. They named the airport after him."

Jashari had been with his family when Serb forces had surrounded his village. At first, the Serbs asked him to surrender, but, when he refused, they fired mortars and tear gas at his home. Jashari and 52 members of his family died in the early hours of 5th March 1998.

The rear of the building was popular with young couples sat kissing on benches, or standing against walls that hid them from view. And at the front of the palace were seven large, yellow letters made from steel. They spelled out the word NEWBORN.

First unveiled on 17th February 2008 – the day Kosovo declared itself independent from Serbia – graffiti covered every inch of the letters. But instead of being vandalism, the graffiti had been produced by thousands of people celebrating the country's independence. Even politicians had scrawled their names onto the massive letters.

I took a photo of Michael sitting inside the letter 'o'. The 9-foot shape dwarfed him. We went to find something to eat.

11

Mayonnaise doesn't sound like the sort of substance that would become my nemesis in Kosovo, but it did.

I cannot pinpoint the exact time when my aversion to the satanic mixture of oil and eggs, masquerading as a sandwich dressing, manifested itself, but in Kosovo, whatever food I ordered, mayonnaise wasn't far behind.

In a cafe we found, I foolishly ordered a hot dog, thinking it would be a bun with a frankfurter in the middle. I was wrong. The round bread cake, with a bit of Balkan sausage inside, was drenched in mayonnaise, the creamy substance coating everything, even splashing out over the side.

"Oh God," I said, shuddering. "I can't eat it." There was no way I could even take a bite of the thing, and so I wrapped it up and pushed it away.

"See what I mean!" said Michael, eating his own hot dog. Mayonnaise was dripping onto his plate. "You're always moaning about food."

"Do you blame me?" I shot back. "It's covered in mayonnaise. I can't stand the stuff."

Still hungry, we found another cafe and sat down. I ordered another hot dog, this time making sure I told the waiter of my special requirement.

"Without mayonnaise," he answered, as he took my order.

I sat back, licking my chops in anticipation of the meal ahead. I was starving, and I knew that Michael was finding the whole situation highly amusing. *That* was annoying me. So as well as museums and photos, I could add *lack of sympathy* to his list of failings.

"Anyway, what's wrong with mayonnaise?" he asked, while we waited.

I shook my head and grimaced. "The taste, the texture, the thought of what it's made of, everything."

Michael smiled and got the guidebook out.

The level of mayonnaise saturation on the new hot dog was worse than the last. Gooey white stuff oozed from the edge of the bread, and made a smacking sound as I tried to prise it open. I cursed mayonnaise to hell, damned its inventor to drown in a vat of his own creation.

"Just tell him you ordered it without mayonnaise," Michael suggested. "It's their mistake, not yours; besides, you must be starving."

I nodded, downtrodden, beaten by a white and creamy foe.

"Without mayonnaise," said the new waiter as he collected my uneaten mayonnaise dog. Remarkably, ten minutes later, a new hot dog arrived, this time free of the evil substance. I devoured it in seconds.

12

With the distant sound of thunder on the horizon, Michael and I took a shortcut through a field pumping with the sounds of crickets. They even drowned out the traffic noises of central Pristina.

In the middle of the waste ground was an abandoned cathedral, just a concrete shell of a church. At the far end of the field lay a set of unattractive tower blocks.

The Serbs had begun constructing the cathedral in 1995, but, when hostilities broke out, work had stopped. Then during the conflict, Albanians living in Pristina began to vandalise it, forcing the UN to step in. They surrounded it with lashings of barbed wire. The wire remains to this day.

"What a shame," I said. "This could be a great church."

"Yeah," agreed Michael, angling for a shot of the barbed wire. "But with most people in Pristina seeing it as a symbol of Milosevic's regime, I doubt it'll ever be finished."

With its congregation of crickets, we left the church, and walked the short distance to the National Library, which was at the other side of the field. It looked like no other library I'd seen. It resembled a megalomaniac's idea of a nuclear bunker.

Its black exterior was covered in some sort of metal netting, and it was topped with a plethora of strange domes. A set of yellow benches around the perimeter provided the only colour.

As we walked around the bizarre building, some students came out of the entrance, chatting and smoking, laughing and joking, Albanian Kosovars who had been small children during the conflict, possibly even displaced at some point in their young lives.

Up a steep road beyond the waste ground was the National Martyrs Monument. After a lung-collapsing trek to it, I was in need of Martyrdom myself, wheezing and coughing like an asthmatic.

Built to commemorate a group of partisans who had died during the Second World War, graffiti covered the monument. The whole place looked sad and abandoned, except for a few well-tended graves nearby. Albanian flags rippled in the air currents close by.

While Michael circled the strange sphere-like object at the centre of the monument, I wandered over to the grave of Ibrahim Rugova, the former president of Kosovo. It looked well-kept with no graffiti anywhere. The grave was white, surrounded by a red rope and golden poles.

Rugova had been the chain smoking, cravat-wearing former leader. Diagnosed with lung cancer at the age of 61, he'd spent his final days furiously puffing way on one cigarette after another, until he finally breathed his last in 2006.

His passing had caused great mourning among his subjects, with people lining the streets of Pristina as his funeral car swept past. Rugova was the man credited with bringing all the different factions involved in the Kosovo crisis together, and it was down to him, say his proud citizens, that an independent nation was made real.

13

The Grand Hotel was a tall concrete block, topped with a neon sign that only illuminated some of the letters at night. While a violent thunderstorm raged outside, Michael and I had no option but to sit in the lobby bar.

Most of our fellow guests looked business-like, all suited up, sitting with laptops. Others looked more casual, probably either journalists or photographers, judging by the bulky bags they carried. Conversation filled the lobby, which was suddenly bolstered by the arrival of a platoon of well-dressed young women. They were tottering about on their heels, shaking umbrellas and straightening hair. Just then, a group of young men arrived and the whole group milled about at one end of the lobby.

"I reckon it's a graduation party," said Michael, staring over at the crowd. "Either that or some rich kid's private birthday bash."

Some of the girls could have been models, and one blonde woman, in particular, looked like pop star, Rita Ora. Ora had been born in Pristina before moving to the UK.

I looked outside at the weather. It was still stormy. The flags outside the entrance were flapping like mad, and rain was smashing against the windowpanes.

"We'll have to brave it," I said, causing Michael to look up from his paperback. "I'm starving. All I've had today is that hotdog and a bit of meagre breakfast in Skopje."

Putting on our jackets, and pulling our hats tight against our heads, Michael and I stepped into the tempest. Litter was ferociously galloping along Mother Teresa Boulevard, and the rain seemed almost horizontal. A jagged line of white flashed from above, briefly illuminating the buildings of Pristina. An unearthly boom closely followed it.

We headed towards a neon pizza sign and took refuge within. It was a small establishment specialising in grasshopper pizzas, but we passed on those and opted for some with tomatoes and mushrooms. Mine came with not a sniff of mayonnaise.

14

The next morning was the final day of our Balkan Odyssey. It was amazing to think that Michael and I had visited every country of the former Yugoslavia, and that, later that evening, we would be flying back to the UK.

It was still raining and windy outside, but the thunderstorm had thankfully gone. Michael and I sat down to have breakfast. "So what's left to see?" I asked, taking a spoonful of yoghurt.

"Not much really," answered Michael, looking at the map of Pristina. "There's a park we could visit, I suppose, but, in this weather, I don't think it's wise."

"Anything else?"

Michael shrugged and looked up. He was smiling.

"What?"

"Well there is *something* we could see, but I'm not sure whether you'll like it..."

"...A museum?"

"What else can we do when it's pouring down?"

"You said no more museums."

"Okay, let's sit in the hotel all morning. That'll be fun."

15

The Ethnographic Museum was not far, but with the rain lashing down, we took a taxi. When we got there, we found the place deserted. After scurrying around trying to find a way in – whilst at the same time attempting to keep the rain at bay – a young woman appeared. She looked at us but said nothing.

Perhaps the taxi driver had dropped us off at the wrong place, I thought. We were inside some sort of walled compound with two buildings. Neither looked like a museum. I was getting wet and annoyed.

"Hello," Michael said to the woman. "Do you speak English?"

The woman nodded, covering her head with one hand to keep her hair dry. "Can I help you?"

"Yes," said Michael. "We're looking for the Ethnographic Museum. Do you know where it is?"

The woman nodded. "Yes, it is here."

After establishing we weren't thieves, the lady told us she was a guide for the museum, but had not expected any visitors due to the rain. "Come," she said. "I will show you."

The woman unlocked the door to one of the buildings, and we followed her in. Just as I'd feared, it was a well-preserved Balkan household filled with pots, pans, and mannequins dressed in old clothes. I felt the urge to bolt, but, with a guide in attendance, this would be highly rude. Instead I forced myself to appear interested.

"These are traditional costumes of women in Western Kosovo," she informed us. "The embroidery with the flowers is a symbol of youth. Please read the information yourselves. It is highly interesting for you, I'm sure."

Michael did so eagerly; I did so under duress. The museum was basically an old house, and my eyes glazed over as soon as I looked at the information sign. Michael was right, I *was* a heathen.

Twenty fun-packed minutes later, we moved on to the second building. The only objects that took my interest were some swords and a gnarled branch that resembled a snake. Outside, after thanking the woman, Michael and I decided to walk back to the hotel. Thankfully, the rain had eased slightly.

"How about another museum?" Michael asked hopefully.

I looked at my watch. We still had plenty of time before we had to go to the airport. "Why not? Let's end the Odyssey with a museum."

16

Half an hour later we were inside the Kosovo Museum, a larger and grander affair than the Ethnographic Museum. It was housed inside a yellow villa that had once been used by the Yugoslav army as their headquarters.

Despite its more exciting exterior, the inside of the Kosovo Museum was another collection of pots and small weapons, but it did house the prized Goddess on a Throne, a 30cm terracotta figurine that was 6000 years old. The Goddess looked like she had her eyes closed and had her hands on her hips. She looked a bit pissed off, actually.

"Look at this," said Michael, reading a caption. I walked over and read it with him. It mentioned a group of barbarians called the *Bastards*. According to the information, this particular tribe liked nothing more than fighting, but, after one particularly fierce battle, the Bastards had been sent packing. Stupid Bastards, I thought to myself.

The lower floor of the museum was a small gallery of photos. As we began perusing them, a man in his late thirties approached us. "Hello," he said. "Welcome to the exhibition."

He turned out to be a tutor to deaf teenagers, teaching them all about photography. The kids in question were all hanging around the periphery of the large room, digital cameras at the ready.

"I am so proud of them," he told us. "They have worked hard for this exhibition." He pointed to a photo showing the lower half of a woman's leg. She was walking a small white dog.

"Please look closely here," he told us. "Can you see where the focus is? It is on the paw of the dog's back leg! And also notice the symmetry of the cobblestones where the line of the woman's leg meets it. Very clever touch."

We moved onto another photograph, and the man gave us another running commentary. It was all quite interesting actually, and I was glad we'd come down. Photography was something I wanted to learn more about.

But then the mood in the museum changed somewhat. Instead of hanging around at the periphery, the man's students suddenly began circling us like paparazzi, snapping off photos left, right and centre.

"I hope you do not mind this," said the man, to an accompaniment of clicks and whirring lenses, "but it is great for my students to see real people enjoying their work. And if you don't mind further, I will move out of the way, so only you will be on their photographs."

It was slightly off-putting to be honest, to be buzzed by cameras from all directions, to be the focus of all this attention, but what could we do? I could now commiserate with famous people, who had to endure this sort of behaviour day in and day out. It made me feel self-conscious, knowing that every move, every facial expression, every turn of my gaze was being recorded in film. But we accepted the attention with good grace, and I made sure I posed thoughtfully at some of the photos, my hand resting on my chin in a most intellectual manner.

17

An hour later, our trip to Pristina, and indeed the Balkans, was over. Michael and I packed our bags, and made sure we had our passports at the ready.

"Verdict?" I asked him as we negotiated a set of road works from the inside of a taxi.

"On Kosovo? Or as a whole?"

"As a whole."

Michael tapped his finger on the door's hand rest. "Well, as a complete trip, I enjoyed the whole lot. Almost everything went according to plan, and the bits that didn't weren't so bad. Even the journey from Montenegro to Albania was okay in the end. But if you want me to rank my top three places, I'd have to say Belgrade was number one, Mostar number two and...maybe Tirana or Skopje number three. What about you?"

"Sarajevo is still my number one – there was just something I love about that place. But then it would be Tirana, I think. Yeah, and then maybe Mostar or Skopje. But I loved Dubrovnik and Bled. They were pretty amazing."

"Oh yeah, I'd almost forgotten about Bled. It seems so long ago. I can't believe it was only two weeks."

We both stared outside at the road works again, thinking our own thoughts. We had seen the beauty of the region, despite its scars of war. We had visited places that many people would not dare to tread, fearful of a war that had ended over a decade previously. Along the way, we had talked to many people, both Muslim and Christian, and found everyone to be equally friendly and hospitable. The former Yugoslavia was a wonderful part of Europe to visit, ripe for new tourists to discover.

The Balkans might still have a way to go to shake off its turbulent past, but, from what Michael and I had seen, it was definitely heading in the right direction. Old towns were being cleaned up and repaired, damaged bridges and bazaars were looking spick and span, and people were proudly walking around their cities and towns with their heads held high.

As we were going through airport security at Pristina's small international airport, a customs man asked me something. "Why you come to Kosovo?"

I looked at the man. Michael had already gone through via a different security booth. I decided to tell the truth. "I came here as a tourist."

The man looked at me for a while, as if searching out the genuineness of my answer. Finally he said, "Do you think you will ever come back?"

"I don't know," I answered. "But I've enjoyed myself in Kosovo, and I think that more people will eventually start coming."

The man nodded, stamped my passport, and handed it back. "Have a good flight back to your home. Kosovo thanks you."

Afterword

I almost didn't write this book.

Not that I didn't want to document our travels around this extraordinary part of Europe. No, the reason for my reticence was that I was scared of what people might think of it.

I'm not talking of the pedant who might notice a passive sentence where an active one would be more suitable, nor am I talking about a person who thinks my prose rambles needlessly. No, I was afraid of how Croatians, Albanians, Serbians, and all the other people who live in the Balkans might react to it.

The Balkan region is home to some of the most nationalistic people on Earth, rightly proud of their heritage, unflappable in their patriotism. But there is also tension and anger, a sad fact that played its part in the Balkan Wars of the 1990s. Ethnic lines were drawn and battle stations commenced. Anybody who has the audacity to write about their nations, their conflicts, their cities and their people is sure to incur some of their wrath too.

For a start, people who live in the Balkans do not really like the term *Balkans*. To them, it conjures negative images of war. For that reason, they prefer the term *Southeast Europe*. To the people of Slovenia, the wealthiest and most northerly of the former Yugoslav republics, they reject the notion that they are even part of Southeast Europe, preferring instead *Central Europe*. Thus, terminology in this region is a minefield. As is the recognition of some of its countries.

Take Kosovo, for instance. Is it an independent country? Or is it part of Serbia? As of July 2013, ninety-eight countries recognise Kosovo as an independent state, which is almost half the world. But more than half the world *does not* recognise Kosovo's independence. I have been careful not to take sides in this book.

I hope what *The Balkan Odyssey* brings to the reader is a sense of adventure, and that travelling to this region can be fun and exciting. What I hope it doesn't do is cause offence.

If it has, then I'm truly sorry.

Other books by the same author:

The Red Quest
Flashpacking through Africa
Take Your Wings and Fly
Temples, Tuk-Tuks and Fried Fish Lips
Panama City to Rio de Janeiro

For more information visit **www.theredquest.com**.

Printed in Great Britain
by Amazon.co.uk, Ltd.,
Marston Gate.